AGENDA

CH00394737

CONTENTS

TWO CHOSEN BROADSHEET POETS

Front cover: C. H. Sisson aged 59, 1973.

Introduction

This tribute to C. H. Sisson is long overdue, not just because his association with *Agenda* goes back nearly to its beginnings, to 1961, when the poem 'Easter' was printed in the magazine, but because an issue devoted to him was to have been edited a few years ago by Betsy Knottenbelt, who was sadly prevented from beginning work on it by her early death in 2005. From Sisson's second full collection, *Numbers* (1965), onwards, every book of his poems includes acknowledgement for work that originally appeared in *Agenda*.

Looking back over his oeuvre, it is hard to think of another contemporary writer whose range is so wide. Many twentieth-century poets have produced important critical writing, and some have also translated extensively. But not many at all have written political and ecclesiastical essays, polemical studies, novels, autobiography, and none, it's safe to say, a study of government as well. What characterizes Sisson's work is that, though the poetry is central to it and provides the strongest continuous thread, he is always striking out in different directions, and poetry is just one mode of inquiry, always an elusive and unreckonable one (for 'poems just happen', as it seemed to him). Partly, this is 'keeping busy', 'passing the time between poems', but for much of his life, despite his early retirement from the civil service at the beginning of 1973, he was extremely busy with what he called 'the conduct of affairs'. These affairs did not stop him from writing, besides an already significant body of poems (collected in *In the Trojan Ditch*), his two published novels, the study of 'British administration', the retrospect on poetry of the first half of the twentieth century, the book dismantling Walter Bagehot, numerous essays, and translations ranging from Virgil's *Eclogues* and Catullus to Heine and Supervielle. The notion that Sisson was a late starter, a notion of which he was fond, is almost a myth. After retirement he basically went on as he always had, adding only editing to his activities, and taking on much larger works as a translator: Lucretius, Dante, the *Aeneid*. Kept up also was an enormous and fascinating correspondence, slivers of which are given here. That his poetry changed, breathed a bit more freely perhaps, was in line with his own commitment to a 'writing of discovery' and to rejecting 'whatever appears with the face of familiarity'. The chronological list of his books printed at the end of the issue gives an idea of the scope and trajectory of this work but not of its remarkable coherence. For range is nothing in itself. It is easy to talk about the breadth of Sisson's work, much harder to pinpoint precisely why it matters. But if we try and do that, it is, for all the interconnectedness of the different kinds of writing, the poetry one is led back to – to what could 'not be said otherwise'.

Though often touted as an 'English' poet, not something he minded exactly, he was more closely involved with foreign literatures and modes than almost any writer one can think of, and translation, far more than being something to pass the time, was a way of extending the reach of his own poems or, as he put it, 'sharpening his literary weapons'. That reminds us of the pointed, cutting nature of most of his writing – it is not a work to feel comfortable in, except occasionally. The essays gathered here attend to that work, but often they attend also to the man who was a lot less forbidding, a lot warmer, than the poems might seem to suggest.

I am grateful to all the contributors (solicited and unsolicited) for what they have done and for being so straightforward, to Michael Schmidt for advice, and to Louise Turner who helped with some of the typing. And of course to Patricia McCarthy and *Agenda*, for allowing this to happen at all and so completing a span of nearly fifty years.

Charlie Louth

C. H. Sisson

On my Fifty-first Birthday

I

Hare in the head-lights dance on your hind legs
Like a poor cat struggling at a rope's end.
Everything is cruelty for innocence.
If you could mark this escape from death
In your thin mind you would have eaten what I have
And, running from form to form, you would consider
The immeasurable benignity of the destructive God.

II

A great sunlit field full of lambs.
The distant perspectives are of the patched earth
With hedges creeping about. If I were to die now
No need of angels to carry me to paradise.
O Lord my God, simplify my existence.

III

The whole hill-side is roofed with lark-song.
What dangerous declivities may I not descend?
It is dark green where the horses feed.
Blackthorn and gorse open before my eyes.

IV

The gulls come inland, alight on the brown land
And bring their sea-cries to this stillness.
It was waves and the surf running they heard before
And now the lark-song and the respiration of leaves.

from *Metamorphoses* (1968)

Robert Wells

C. H. Sisson – A Memoir

It was in *Agenda* that I first came across the name C. H. Sisson and read a
poem by him. The poem was 'Numbers'. I have the issue in front of me,
stapled and in a matt yellow cover (not the sleekly bound and weighty affair
which *Agenda* has become, but still keeping its youthful slightness). It is
dated Dec 1963/Jan 1964, Vol 3 No 3. I remember the moment of discovery
and my surprised delight at the poem, its compound of shapeliness and
irregularity, directness and obscurity; the animus of its tone, in which lyrical
response and disenchantment were mixed; and the puzzling, fragmented
portrait which it presented of a mind which at once doubted itself and was
confidently distinct. It wasn't like anything else that I had met in contemporary
verse, but it wasn't eccentric either. The words seemed to be spoken directly
onto the page; they were not listening to themselves, or covertly inviting
admiration. At the age I then was (the date tells me I was sixteen), one pores
over such discoveries as rarely afterwards, and yet often fails to follow them
up. Other interests supervened. But I remembered the poem and the name.
I saw it again above a clutch of poems in the magazine *X*, and found it too
under the long epigraph in Geoffrey Hill's *Mercian Hymns*, a position of
honour which gave it, in my eyes, a legendary aura. Sisson, it appeared from
this forbidding passage (the opening paragraph, as I was later to discover,
of 'Native Ruminations'), was unexpectedly taken up with matters other
than poetry. How could that be? I also recall turning over the pages of his
third volume of poems, *Metamorphoses*, in a bookshop one day, but being
put off by the title poem – which I still rather dislike – as well as by the
physical appearance of the book. But when, ten years after my encounter
with the poem in *Agenda* (while sitting in a room in Tehran, looking out at
a snowbound garden and at a persimmon tree, its leafless branches vividly
stuck with fruit, and glancing at a month-old copy of *The Listener*) I lighted
upon Donald Davie's review of *In the Trojan Ditch*, with its boldly trenchant
declaration: 'It is years since there appeared a book of poems to equal this
one for seriousness and accomplishment, and the unadvertised drama which
is acted out on its pages', I knew the name at once and longed to see the
book. I could believe the phrase 'unadvertised drama' (though I see now that
Davie, in praising, was, as always, taking a swipe at others too). And there
was also a reference to a 'great' poem, 'The Usk', which was bound to whet
my appetite. What could the poem be, for which Davie stuck out his neck so
forthrightly? I knew that, among the first things I had to do when I got back to

England was to get hold of a copy of this book. I did (almost at once I bought two more, which I sent to friends), and read it with passionate enthusiasm on the floor of my Finchley Road bedsit.

I rehearse these incidents, slight as they are, because they are straws in the wind, of the kind which help to determine a life; looked back on, they make their own sense as part of a story. Two years later I found myself outside Taunton Station, in the company of Michael Schmidt, nervously shaking hands with a vigorous white-haired man in his early sixties, who turned out to be not the angry Timon whom I half-expected, but courteous, eager and a bit awkward in manner, drily humorous, and as I discovered when we got back to his house in Langport, a most considerately hospitable person – in this, his wife Nora played an equal part. Sisson was a forceful man, but that was something one found out. He didn't impose himself. There is a passage in his novel, *One Eye on India* (the protagonist, Pearce, is himself) which sums this up:

That rawest youth in which one is tempted to protest to all comers that one is such and such, but in fact conceals much, was away in the dim past. Pearce now wished to conceal nothing and to display nothing. What would be the use? For we are to people what they comprehend; it is a vanity to wish to be known…. There are those who are aware of their own existence only in the imagined opinions of others; these are the people who are dominated by fear.

Sisson, you knew on meeting him, was not of their number.

*

Over the years, I visited Charles (as I learned to call him) and Nora perhaps six or seven times. What did a visit consist of? Though Sisson's poems bear witness to an incurable distress, an *angoisse* running beneath everything else, he knew how to live with and manage it – a Philoctetes who had domesticated his wound so that it hardly appeared. He was pleased with, and proud of, his house, his garden, the great view out over often flooded fields to the Dorset hills in the distance ('You could look out on worse than that', he said to me once, half-gesturing towards it on a day when it lay spread out with even more than usual splendour). He had the unobtrusive pride and independent spirit of a man who has come a long way from very little, with no one to help him, and who takes nothing in his modest prosperity for granted. A guest, arriving, would be offered (with the self-deprecating trace of a smile) 'a look round the estate' by which he meant the carefully kept stretch of garden behind his

10

house, on an escarpment of the River Parrett. Here were the small fishpond he had built, the espaliered plum trees, the mulberry tree, the medlar, the herb-garden and vegetable beds off to one side (among the vegetables, the artichokes were his special pride – irregularly-shaped, full of taste, hard to digest, and superseded historically by the blander potato, they reminded me of his poems), the apple tree with its mistletoe, all of which he had planted and which appear in poem after poem, less as their subject (he could never rest for long in the outward appearances of things) than caught up with and tangled in his meditation. They are there most memorably in the last section of 'Burrington Combe', one of the high points of his poetry, which I hold back from quoting because it would have to be given entire. (One of Sisson's obstinacies was to refuse, or so he claimed, to have any plant in his garden which had been introduced into England after the seventeenth century.) These things might not cure Sisson's restlessness, but he was far from being above enjoying the Horatian contentment which they allowed him to represent to himself. There is the poem which opens, 'Am I not fortunate in my garden?' and the one which concludes, 'There are worse things than becoming a house'. There is also an off-handedly acute poem addressed to Horace, in which he calls into question Horace's contentment and the finality of his art, while admiring both. He challenges Horace: 'Were there not other poets, if you think carefully?' – poets, that is, rough and discontented, who were no part of the Augustan settlement, and who have not survived. It is a question which true admirers of the 'monumentum aere perennius' are bound to put to themselves. And it is with these lost poets that Sisson counts himself:

> Teach me to bury my voice in a dead woodland
> It is better not to be heard
> Than to speak forever.

'My living', he explains, 'has come too hard'.

A further part of the visit was to be driven to some of the sites and scenes nearby which also appear in the poems. There were the Somerset Levels, where Sisson owned a couple of fields, which he let out for grazing to a farmer. Once a year he would meet the farmer to negotiate the letting, a meeting he looked forward to and relished as belonging to what he unashamedly called 'real life', the life which he himself remembered from childhood holidays (as in his poem, 'Ellick Farm') and which reached him through his mother, the daughter of a tenant farmer, who kept in her voice 'the faint intonation and marked rhythms of West Country speech'. Or one might be taken to a small stretch of woodland, lost in the larger woodland surrounding it, which he owned, where he would sometimes come for the pleasure of sitting and

11

strolling there. Of William Barnes, Sisson wrote, 'for him the first meaning of "our own free land" is the few fields a man may manage to own, as in his Dorchester days he bought a few symbolic acres at Bagber' (Bagber was Barnes's birthplace). Sisson's bit of woodland and couple of fields were symbolic in the same way. Another stop was Aller church. Here the defeated Danish king, Guthrum, had been entertained by King Alfred and had been baptized. The lines of the landscape in its disposition about the church make this an almost ideally beautiful place, even if it were not for the historical association. For Sisson, though he only spoke glancingly of such feelings (he was never intrusively strident or doctrinaire in conversation, though he didn't hide his loyalties or his prejudices), it was a place where a lost England might be, if not recovered in imagination, at least felt in the loss. 'When shall I see England again?' he asks in the little poem 'Aller Church'. Athelney and Sedgemoor were also part of the circuit. Then there was the walk along the bank of the Parrett, within a stone-throw of his house, this too the scene or starting point for several poems. 'O river who wind away from view...'

*

Sisson's house was ordered and comfortable, the comfort being of a spare, unindulgent kind. There was no clutter, and I remember no bright colours either. It was a place of set mealtimes, where the chores were divided and promptly done, and a steady routine of work adhered to (which was put aside for guests). Work was Sisson's way of coping with his inherent restlessness or *angoisse*, and with a mind that preyed on itself at once unless given tasks – the constant reviewing, the translations of Virgil and Dante. (The Dante weighed on him and he grew impatient with the *Paradiso* – I recall him making some reference to being dazzled by the over-bright neon strip-lighting of Dante's Heaven.) In an early poem, 'Thomas de Quincey', he writes, 'Of course it was stupor that he wanted/But his mind would work'. This last line always recurs to me when I read Sisson or think of him. It was as if there was a radioactive coal within his mind which wouldn't be put out or turned off. There was also a compulsive habit of ratiocination by which he worked his way ineluctably (a favourite word with him) into positions which, right or wrong, might be narrowly contrary and difficult, as if he needed to entrap or confine himself. One can feel this happening in 'Native Ruminations', in his over-ingeniously mechanical poem 'The Discarnation', or in the sympathy shown in his essays to the extreme scruples of such figures as Christina Rossetti or A. E. Housman, or indeed the non-juring bishops who refused to renege on their oath of allegiance to James II. It is striking that two figures to whom Sisson early attached himself, Ezra Pound and Charles Maurras, tended, from a

12

narrow base and by a relentless logic of their own, to work themselves into impossible positions; and that both, out of a misconceived patriotism, later ended up on trial for their lives as traitors to their country. (Both were also revealed as virulent anti-Semites; Sisson had no truck at all with this, but in drawing attention to what he considers valuable or interesting in the work of both men, he attempts, surely mistakenly, to pass over in silence what must remain an inseparably vitiating element in it.)

Sisson's imagination is drawn by ideas and images of constraint. In politics he is for Filmer over Locke. Poetic composition is, for him, an essentially involuntary process; and this holds true also for his version of the history of poetic technique (expounded, for example, in the review/essay 'Poetry and Sincerity') – that in any given period there is no choice but to write in a given way. The need for constraint, the bridling at what are taken as pretensions to freedom, smacks very strongly of a Calvinistic determinism. This appears most obviously in his preference – in the arrangement of *In the Trojan Ditch*, in *Christopher Homm*, and in *On the Lookout* – for telling a story backwards, proceeding not from the past towards an open future but from a predestined present back into a fixed and narrowing past. There was something stern and gaunt in the tenor of Sisson's life, some lack or unfulfilment ('The best word here is Starve') which his poems constantly return to, and which made itself felt in him, without ever compromising the friendliness and consideration, like the cold edge to a warm autumn day. It must have been this lack which he translated into his hunger for language, by which his writing was driven.

There were a few striking works of art in Sisson's house, drawings and paintings by modernists and contemporaries. These works were akin in sensibility to his poems, and resolutely modern in their refusal of a conventional or easy beauty. But the most revealing object was an ancient one, a piece of mediaeval stonework, the keystone to a small arch, the boss of which had been carved into a man's head, the mouth wide open, and the entire head seeming to consist of, to be be reduced to, the man's cry. Sisson produced this object on one of my visits – it was a recent acquisition – inviting me to share his pleasure in it. I could not. It was too stark, too shockingly expressive. Yet what it revealed was what I recognized in his poetry – the need to put words to what issued from that gaping mouth, to articulate the cry. In the first chapter of his *English Poetry 1900-1950* (a brilliantly entertaining and out-of-the-way assessment, which has not had its due), Sisson writes of the scholar A.H. Bullen, whom he rescues deservedly from obscurity on the strength of a handful of outstanding epigrams: 'It could not be said that he did not speak out before he died, and that is all anybody can do'. To speak out – that was what counted for Sisson in poetry; and that the speech, to authenticate it, should keep something of the cry's rough helplessness and

13

vehemence. Thinking of that gargoyle head, I think too of his little poem, 'The Goldfish' (a sort of epitaph on a casualty of his garden pond, perhaps – a small domestic observation, yet immense in its reach):

Everything that is beautiful must be taken away
As that goldfish was. Shining, and plated with gold,
Its mouth trembling, its eye stony with solicitude
– I gasped when I saw it; it was my own cry.

*

Where should the limit be drawn with inconsequential memories and reflections? It seems to me significant that I don't remember Sisson ever listening to recorded music – that must have gone against the grain. But he had, as a young man, taught himself the recorder, to be able to play Elizabethan songs. No gramophone then; certainly no television; yet he was a confirmed listener to radio news bulletins and follower of current affairs (not a phrase I imagine him liking), and would keep up a caustic commentary, over coffee in the kitchen, or while washing up, on the assumptions and presumptions of the commentators. I remember also how, unlike many poets, he was a good driver. He must have learnt to drive on army jeeps in India during the war; in any case, it was part of the general competence in practical affairs that he expected of himself; and while he was at the wheel there would be a similarly caustic commentary on the behaviour of others on the road. But caustic as the commentary tended to be in such matters, he was accepting of, and uncensorious about, shortcomings. He was the least self-righteous of men, and didn't call others fools without counting himself one too ('Such a fool as I am you had better ignore'). Our conversation once turned, for some reason, to burials in Westminster Abbey, and I recalled an anecdote about the painter Kneller, who when this honour was proposed had exclaimed, 'They do bury fools there!' – to which Sisson briskly rejoined that this was true of every church and graveyard.

I loved to look at the books in Sisson's house, and on his shelves I first discovered various books which I afterwards found and bought for myself. While I was engaged on a translation of Virgil's *Georgics* (Sisson told me with some regret that I had beaten him to it), he fetched out and showed me Martyn's mid-eighteenth-century edition, asking me if I knew of it. In this case, I did. It was, with its practical sense and excellently plain prose translation (Martyn was a botanist first, and a classicist second), already my secret weapon. But that is an indication of how well equipped he was and how able accurately to identify what was required for such a task. On another

14

occasion, taken aback that I had not read it, he lent me Fenollosa's essay on the Chinese written character – the crucial modernist critical text for poetry, as he considered it. But it was the way his books belonged together which chiefly drew me. They were never the trophies of a bibliophile nor ivory-tower fortifications (not that I would slight these), but all for use, and a part of his life. He once said teasingly to an academic of his acquaintance, whose credentials for the role of Moral Tutor to his students he doubted, 'You'd learn more from half-an-hour spent digging in your garden than from all your books!' In *On the Lookout*, he recalls how, as a young boy, he would linger by the twopenny tray outside a bookshop in Bristol, which he had just time to reach in his school lunch-hour, if he hurried, and he describes a few of the purchases he managed to afford, among them a selection of Malory (the recollection of which perhaps surfaces in one of his finest poems, 'In Flood'). Of secondhand bookshops he adds, 'Here I move as an expert'. And it was true. He knew in a moment if it was worth lingering or not. I remember him stepping into Shakespeare & Co. in Paris, in its dispiriting modern reincarnation, and stepping right back out again. I remember too an occasion in Dorchester when, on our entry, the proprietress of the shop, looking up, muttered quite loudly under her breath the word 'incorrigible' (there must have been some previous incident). On this occasion he noticed in the corner of a shelf an old Bohn edition of Jeremy Taylor's *Holy Living and Holy Dying*, and pointing it out to me, asked if I had a copy. I didn't. 'Well', he said, 'it teaches you how to live, and how to die... and at 40p., that's cheap.' I never catch sight of this copy on my shelves without thinking of his testimonial and the playfully tentative flicker of a smile with which it was delivered. It was the particular quality of Sisson's jokes (he was a very funny man), giving them their charm as well as their force, that they arose directly out of his deeper concerns.

*

It is easy to forget, when confronted by the bulk of Sisson's work, how very little of it belongs to the earlier part of a long life. His poem 'On my Fifty-first Birthday' occurs on page 112 of a *Collected Poems* over five hundred pages long. By the time we get to the end of the poems which had made up *In the Trojan Ditch* we are still only at page 186, and he is sixty and retired. He already describes that volume, in the Foreword, as consisting for the most part of 'poems of the return journey'. Until that time his writing life had been in extreme tension with the heavy demands and powerful ambitions, finally disappointed, of a professional life which had brought him very near to the top of the Civil Service – a tension which can be felt acutely in the poems and which must at times have been almost uncontainable. It has a particular force, exacerbated by the sense of life missed or grasped at too late, as it discharges itself in the Provençal sequence, written directly after his retirement, which opens *Anchises*; the voice in 'Cotignac' is that of a man very narrowly skirting breakdown.

The greater part of Sisson's poetry belongs to the period of his old age – the time when most poets have had their say and the best of their work is behind them. Old age is what Sisson's poems document – old age itself and his life looked back on from old age. The subject is a relatively uncommon one, being that part of the human lot which poetry tends to overlook, and it is a great part of Sisson's distinction that he does not. Hardy, in whose *Collected Poems* a similar imbalance occurs, is his peer in this. In his essay on Barnes, Sisson quotes Malherbe on the continuing favours of the Muse in old age:

> Je les possédai, jeune, et les possède encore
> A la fin de mes jours,

lines which must have been in his mind where his own writing too was concerned. But if poetry was necessary to him as a way of easing his mind, it remained just that, a necessity, an exaction (as the title of his best single volume, *Exactions*, confirms). He never, I think, refers to it as a consolation; it was too close to *angoisse*. Poetry as he practised it was more voice than art; it was the Sibyl, 'speaking any words / Wildly', rather than the Horatian *monumentum* in which another temperament might have found repose. As poet, he comes before us as 'The messenger of anything I say', as he puts it in 'The Usk'. In an introduction to the writings of Philip Mairet, Sisson comments:

> Old age is hardly a time to be recommended, but Mairet was one of those rare people in whom it did involve a certain flowering. He was one of those for whom 'The soul's dark cottage, battered and decayed' really did 'let in new light through chinks that time has made'.

Would Sisson have allowed that 'a certain flowering' occurred for him too, or that Waller's lines might apply in his case? Echoing Landor, he inscribed his last book, *What and Who*, for me, 'fruit from an old tree'.

*

These reflections on the theme of old age in Sisson's poetry arise for me now from a memory of his turning to me, as we stood under the mulberry

16

tree at the bottom of his garden, and saying with his usual slight smile and suppressed vehemence that the Psalmist had got it right.

The days of our age are threescore years and ten; and though men be so strong, that they come to fourscore years: yet is their strength but labour and sorrow; so soon it passeth away, and we are gone.

Later I climbed into the mulberry tree to gather the fruit he was no longer able to gather himself. That was not the only time I heard him quoting the Psalmist. In his last years he would speak matter-of-factly about wanting to die. I remember him describing the visit of a well-meaning vicar ('an inoffensive little man... well, a little man'): 'He asked me what I was looking forward to. Well, what could I reply? I told him I was looking forward to Death'. (Bland clergymen, and those with a line in easy uplift, were an especial bugbear of his – as in 'A Letter to John Donne', *the tour-de-force* among his early poems.) Sisson's final *Collected Poems* came out some months after he had suffered an enfeebling stroke. (It is badly proofed as a result, but he was never meticulous in this respect; the kinds of accuracy he cared about were different.) Visiting him soon afterwards, I found him standing, diminished, by the bus-stop in Langport, having come down the hill from his house to meet me in obedience to the doctor's prescription that he should walk. I recall our slow return, his speech now very hard to follow. (It was always hard to catch at the best of times, since he spoke in a throwaway rather mumbled manner, at once gruff and diffident, as if turning away from his words in the act of speaking them – just as his poems often turn away from their form while it is still barely established.) We made the usual round of the garden, which he was no longer able to work in. He gestured to the now overrun herb-garden, 'More of a herb-wilderness!' (Herbs, in Sisson's poetry, serve as an emblem of an earthliness that is free of taint, a kind of heavenly foretaste:

The scent of thyme, never off my hands
Except when rue chases it, or fennel or sage...)

A deprivation he particularly resented was his inability to drive, since he was now unable to do the round of the loved places near his home. I asked him if there were any more poems. 'All that is past,' he replied, 'there's nothing now' – as if the remark had a wider reference. The 'Finale' in the *Collected Poems*, the last of many, is what it purports to be.

After this I made one more visit, in the year before he and Nora died. I have a last memory of them both standing in the corridor by the open front-door to say goodbye, tired by my visit (which was brief, though I had lingered too long in the garden) and of her saying to him, with the cheerful wit which was peculiarly hers, 'You lean on this wall, Charles, and I'll lean on that one.' Recalling that remark, the seemingly innocent humour of it and the clear quavering voice in which it was delivered, I remember another remark of hers, which, for anyone who has recoiled from the negative charge which runs through Sisson's work, will appear, as I am (almost) sure she meant it to be, shockingly funny: 'I always tell Charles', she declared over the dinner-table after some blackly sweeping comment of his, 'that he should try to *look on the bright side*.' When I next came back to Langport, it was for Sisson's funeral. It had always been a joke which he relished – the distrust with which the good people of Langport, himself included, regarded the wicked people of Huish Episcopi, the directly adjoining parish. But since there are no more burials in Langport church, it was to Huish Episcopi churchyard that we came, after five minutes' walk down a blustery road in the autumn sunshine, to see him into the ground.

Two years afterwards I found myself writing the entry on Sisson for the *Dictionary of National Biography*. It is a salutary exercise to sum up the life and work of a man one has known, particularly when these are so full and various, in two thousand words, and to do so justly. Once the main facts are rehearsed, the titles of the chief works given, there is only space for the briefest description and judgement. The greater part of the carefully assembled materials goes out of the window, and what is left is compact and tidy as a little urn. Thoughts crowd in of the shortness even of a long life, of the little space there is in a life, and of the imperfect way we make use of that little space – the more so, given that such thoughts are the stuff of Sisson's poetry. The living process had suddenly turned into the fixed record. For oneself too, the straws in the wind are no longer that. I am now at the age Sisson was, when, looking out at the persimmon tree in the Tehran garden and lighting upon Davie's review, I recognized the name I had first encountered in *Agenda*. Forty-five years after that encounter, the tenuously-drawn circle is completed, as I put together these inchoate reflections for the same magazine.

*

I should perhaps leave it there, but find that I have much to add. Among the literary reasons for the attraction which Sisson's poetry held for me, there is, I now realize, one closer to home. Sisson belonged to the same generation as my father and came from a similar background. Both were the sons of artisans (Sisson's father kept a clock-and-watch repair shop, though he later qualified as an optician; my own father's father was an electrician)

18

and were raised in impoverished lower-middle-class households – the class which, in Sisson's view, contained the essential strength of England. In such households jam on bread was a Sunday treat, and the only fruit ever seen had been sold cheap because it was bruised or over-ripe. Both grew up in southern provincial cities (Sisson in Bristol, my father in Southampton) but spent some holidays on farms, one parent being from the country, so that a rural connection made itself felt. Both were bookish boys, possessed by a passion for language. They made their way by brain-power and such scholarships as were available, with no money to back them up and no one conveniently placed to put in a word for them (on this subject read Sisson's coruscatingly funny review of Lord Redcliffe-Maud's autobiography, *Experiences of an Optimist*, reprinted in *Anglican Essays* under the title 'The Company he Keeps'). In one respect my father was luckier than Sisson – when he won a scholarship to the local grammar school he was able to take it up, as Sisson was not (Sisson's parents feared that they would be unable to afford the school uniform). That meant that my father reached Oxford, as Sisson should have and did not. It also meant, to his great regret later on, that he had no knowledge of Greek. There are further similarities. Both my father and Sisson spent time in Germany in the early 1930s. They experienced at first hand the menace of Nazism. (Both heard Hitler speak, saw him close to, and testified to the extraordinary power of his rhetoric.) Both recoiled disgustedly and with an innate decency from the experience, the shock remaining with them through life. Yet both were proofed by their background against a Marxist reaction, the theoretical preserve, as far as they were concerned, of *bien-pensant* contemporaries, expensively educated and a few years older than themselves, by whom they did not care to be patronized. As Sisson wrote, again of Barnes, 'The lowest middle classes have always lacked sentiment about the condition of the workers. They understand the troubles of poverty too well.'

Sisson's sympathies, like my father's, were by inclination with the other ranks, rather than with the officers, and there was something in their sense of humour, observant and drily unillusioned, which was also of the other ranks. Sisson's *Collected Poems* opens emblematically with the poem 'On a Troopship'; and he records, as proudly as any other eminence he achieved, the fact that he rose to the rank of sergeant during his war service in India. It is something to be able to set Kipling right, where technicalities of language are involved. But that is what Sisson authoritatively does, when writing on him in *English Poetry 1900-1950*. Quoting a passage of Kipling's verse, he comments, 'It is not in this tone that troops speak of a mutiny', and adds: 'his view of the British soldier is always that of the outsider.' Perhaps he has poked his nose into sergeants' messes, but it is evident that he has never moved at ease in those exclusive circles.'

Also in this connection, Sisson once told me that the people he felt closest to in his professional life at the Ministry of Labour, where he was responsible for much post-war safety-at-work legislation, were the older generation of trade union officials with whom he dealt.

It seems to me too that there was a similarity in the accommodation which Sisson and my father made with life, after the interruption of war, in the narrowed decade of the fifties, my father in the academy as a Classics don (specializing – another likeness – in Horace and Lucretius, and the variable rules governing Latin prose rhythm), Sisson in the Civil Service – an accommodation which began to come apart in the middle years of the sixties, my father dying prematurely, and Sisson, the more robust man by far, retiring prematurely, to set out undividedly on the literary trajectory which had always been his first inclination. (The manner of his retiring was typical of him. Having rocked the boat and been promoted out of harm's way, he used the opportunity of an administrative reform with which he had been charged to abolish his own job.) What all this amounts to saying is that Sisson speaks for the world out of which my father came as no other poet does, and that there is something in his voice, over and above the shared characteristics I have identified, which I recognize and respond to, because at a remove it speaks for me as well.

*

But when I have to make a case for Sisson's poetry, to show what I find compelling about it, so as to win over a doubter, I'm always puzzled. People either get it or they don't, and if they don't, an attempted demonstration doesn't help much. The poetry gives next to nothing to hold on to: 'I speak too plain / Yet not so plain as to be understood' – 'The Usk' again. There is no luxuriance, no welcomingly substantial texture of word and image. Metaphors are few. Outstanding poems, such as 'The Red Admiral', 'In Flood', even 'Taxila' (which centres on an anecdote), once you examine them, seem to consist of almost nothing, barely to hold together, the minimum of gesture being made for the form to be achieved – and that is precisely their virtue. What attracts me above all in Sisson's poetry is a quality of mind which depends on, and takes the risk of, cutting through as directly as it can to what is essential in what it has to say. I find this exhilarating partly because it is so different from my own way of proceeding in poetry. For me poetry is in the making, first of all. For Sisson (I come back to this) it is, first of all, in the speaking out. The two ways – that of the oracle or prophet, and that of the humbler craftsman – are not mutually exclusive, of course. Both are bent on finding the right words, and each needs the other.

Sisson's instinct for identifying the essential and going straight for it was characteristic of the man no less than of the poetry. Since this is a memoir, I would like to illustrate it by two anecdotes, rather than by turning to the poems. The first concerns Sisson's life in the Civil Service and was told me by himself. Two departments had been amalgamated into one, of which he found himself in charge. As a consequence of the amalgamation some unforeseen anomalies had arisen in the pay of the employees. Sisson set a subordinate to investigate these and report back to him. The subordinate, who was conscientious to a fault, laboured at the task and at last submitted an immensely long and intricate paper, covering every last eventuality, hypothesis and possibility of solution. When Sisson received the document his heart sank; he glanced over its many pages, then simply wrote across the top the key question, the only one which counted, 'Has anyone been underpaid?', and handed it back. He told this story not in his own praise (that wasn't his habit) but as an illustration of misdirected meticulousness and elaboration. Years later, the subordinate reminded him of this incident, telling him with gratitude how he had been freed and helped in his work as a result. I feel something of the same gratitude towards Sisson's poetry, which is often, in relation to its own confusions (and, in its satirical passages, to the confusions of contemporary cant) like that scrawled question across the top of the report.

The second anecdote comes from Nora, though now I am uncertain whether I had it from her or secondhand. Sisson had been visiting the grave of Henry Vaughan; coming afterwards to the River Usk at a place where it ran into pools, and much moved by the place and its associations, he set Nora to stand guard, and, throwing off his clothes, walked straight into the river, up to his neck ('You flow like the truth, river, I will get in/Over me, through me ...'). That night he wrote 'The Usk'. The story shows Sisson at his best, in his poetry too. He is the man who walks straight into the river.

*

The mixture of clarity and confusion which first struck me in 'Numbers' and which 'The Usk' dramatizes is a centrally distinctive feature of Sisson's poetry. 'River let me be crystalline' competes with 'It is confusion and a madman's tongue'. The combination is implied, in a telling conceit, in 'Catullus' (the poem which prefaces Sisson's translation):

His mind was a clear lake in which he had swum:
There was nothing now but to await a new cloud.

21

The 'clear lake' here is hardly a metaphor. It is Lake Garda, surrounding the peninsula of Catullus's Sirmio. But the 'new cloud' means the coming of Christ (born fifty years or so after the death of Catullus). The lines, with those that follow, brilliantly represent the meeting in European culture of the classical and the Christian. Sisson's poetry is both 'clear lake' and 'new cloud'. The roughness or awkwardness of manner belonging to the confusion goes far deeper than mere truculence. Yet to some degree it is the prevalent manner of the 1940s generation of poets to whom David Wright introduced Sisson – the counterpart in verse of their determinedly unruly lives, their way of letting you know (in case you had been under any illusion on this score) that they are no gentlemen. Sisson enjoyed the comedy of the contrast between his ordered existence and theirs; he knew that their makeshift bohemianism was not for him in life, but he did practise it, even to the point of affectation sometimes, in his verse. I would like to insist here, by contrast, on the qualities by which the roughness and awkwardness are complemented in his work – the elegance, concision and enigmatic felicity of the classical epigrammatist. An early example (apart from 'Numbers' itself) is 'Christmas at the Greyhound':

'All strangers now; there is nobody that I know.'
Draw near to the hearth; there is one nature of fire.

This beautifully compact exchange might have come, in translation, straight out of the Greek Anthology. Similar instances are scattered throughout the *Collected Poems*, and though this epigrammatic element has been little noticed, it plays an essential part in determining the character of the work. It recurs in such later poems (which could not have come out of the Greek Anthology) as this, from the 'Sequelae' sequence:

I have seen the mallard fly out of the rhine,
The snipe skip round the willow and then away;
Nothing to be touched, O the creation my friend
And the dawn will rise upon a cold field.

('Rhine', according to the dictionary, is a South-West dialect word meaning 'large open ditch'.) That suddenly exclaimed 'O the creation my friend' is the always implied, rarely expressed, positive which accompanies, as its other face, the refusal of which we are more usually aware in Sisson's work. The creation is his friend because he imagines himself as having disappeared into it, the dawn rising upon a field where, we understand, he is no longer to be found. The troubled consciousness which has sullied creation, which

22

has intruded upon the cold field, is now (in the concluding phrase of 'In Flood') 'in place', or is for a moment so effaced that it can imagine its own disappearance to the point of living it.

Where the peculiar directness of Sisson's poetry is concerned, a further observation may be helpful. His insistence that the language of poetry must be the language of conversation reaches beyond any mere aesthetic preference for one style over another. We exist, Sisson believed, not as 'individuals' but only in relation to one another – as part of a historic community, a congregation, the relation being proved by language, our ability to speak to and understand each other. When this language is destroyed or abandoned, and the possibility of shared speech disappears, then we ourselves disappear with it. 'Without congregation', he writes in 'Native Ruminations', 'there is no meaning.' Without the conversation by which the meaning is proved, there can be no 'you' or 'I'. In that case we are reduced to the condition of the 'ghost among ghosts' in 'Est in conspectu Tenedos', or of the wandering refugee Anchises, since the Troy in whose existence we too existed has fallen. Sisson said magnificently (in a radio interview with Clive Wilmer), 'Poetry is the nearest we come to human speech'. It must necessarily consist of the language of conversation.

*

Even in my first enthusiasm, I was never able to swallow Sisson whole. In particular I found the self-disgust hard to take – as it always is whether in a person or a piece of writing, when one cannot see a justification for it. It comes over embarrassingly as a kind of self-indulgence, a covert aggression. The emotion is genuine, but the form it takes is somehow not. I am reminded of T. S. Eliot's remark about *Hamlet*, that it is 'full of some stuff that the writer could not drag to light, contemplate, or manipulate into art', and of Hamlet the man, that he 'is dominated by an emotion which is inexpressible, because it is in *excess* of the facts as they appear.' The disgust which Sisson expresses is often accompanied, particularly in some early poems, by an attempt at brutal plain-speaking, which also misfires. (In this respect only, I think, we do sometimes catch the poetry listening to itself with an eye to the effect upon us.) In the 1950s this straining for effect may have passed for bold; but it now seems, and even seemed to me on first reading, off-target, a bit callow. Here again, Sisson's desire to let us know that he is not half so respectable as he might appear smacks of those poets, George Barker and others, whom he met in the pub with David Wright. Are we really supposed to be shaken when a newspaper is referred to as 'bum-paper'? Is it such an outrage (*pace* St. Paul) if, when someone attractive walks by, we turn our

23

heads and look? If all sex is 'lechery' or 'fornication', what words are left, when we need them, for real instances of grief and exploitation? And what has become of happiness? That too, after all, is a reality. Sisson sometimes writes of the living body as if it were an already noisome corpse. There are moments in *Christopher Homm* which verge on the pathological, where far from representing the human condition, he seems to be claiming some perversely special status for his put-upon protagonist. I have to admit (as my references to Timon and Philoctetes suggest) that, when I first met Sisson, it came as something of a surprise to me, innocently literal as my reading had been, to discover that he was, in his first old age, rather a handsome-looking man and of a robustly healthy appearance. Nature had not been unkind to him (though it should never be forgotten that it had been terribly unkind to his disabled young sister, a girl 'on the verge of imbecility', the companion and playmate of his boyhood, whom he loved and who died when he was fourteen – an event commemorated with desperate tenderness in his poem 'Remembering the Dead'). Sisson's poetry is nothing if not carnal. The body is everywhere in it, yet he can't allow himself to take pleasure in the body without immediately seeking refuge in self-punishment.

With the self-disgust goes a disappointment which is sometimes specific, as he reflects on wrong turnings taken or possibilities unrealized, sometimes general as he reflects that all turnings are wrong, all possibilities delusions. Sisson protests an admiration for Roman virtue ('No hurt because the lips are tight'), but an air of complaint, too often renewed, hangs about some of the poems, and begins to seem merely habitual. Of course, all he is doing is having yet another go at writing the same poem; or else he is writing, section by section, the same poem – the portrait of a mind and its contents (as in 'Numbers', but without the stringency), where the truth of the representation is all and no other discriminations apply (as we have become used to the convention, and too accepting of it, in Pound's *Cantos*, John Ashbery's lucubrations, Robert Lowell's 'sonnets' and the later poems of Geoffrey Hill). The accumulation tells against him. This was something he very well knew, yet the knowledge merely becomes part of the complaint, a further twist to it. There is a limit, too, one set rather low, to the number of times a poet can tell us that we should take no notice of him, or that it would have been better if he had kept his mouth shut. And again, if everything is wrong even at best, what words are left for the real losses and misfortunes of life? Is there any reader of Sisson among his admirers who does not feel some impatience in this respect? I happened to see the letter which Davie wrote to him on the publication of *Anchises*. It was mainly congratulatory (Davie especially liked 'Ulysses', a real 'humdinger' as he described it – a word which sounded improbable on Davie's lips), but he identified and took exception to the self-pity. I remember too how, after a

24

reading of Sisson's in Cambridge, a distinguished poet then living in Cambridge, a friend and admirer of his, came up to him afterwards and said affectionately, 'You're a gloomy old bugger!' (or was it 'sour' rather than 'gloomy'?). Neither Davie nor this Cambridge poet could be considered any slouch himself in the matter of gloom. When we find them both suggesting that Sisson is laying it on a bit thick, and (with Nora) that it wouldn't hurt to 'look on the bright side', we know, if we didn't already, that something is awry.

Sisson's best poems by far are those where the inner is balanced by the outer world, and where the appearances of things or accounts of people and events hold the downward drag of his meditation in check – poems where we get 'the red admiral' as well as 'but let the meaning go'. That is why *Night Thoughts and Other Chronicles*, a series of autobiographical reminiscences, is one of his strongest performances. It is a particular strength of the finest of the early poems, which, in their hard specificity, 'take a matter so far, and no further', as he once phrased it to me.

Though Sisson would have disliked the comparison, the element of aggressive self-disgust and the allied sense of disappointment, of missed chances, in his work is very close to that which reveals itself in the work of Philip Larkin and others of Larkin's generation. In a different manifestation it can be found too in the masochistic bohemianism of the 1940s poets. A generation further back the phenomenon recurs, rancorously forceful, in that formidable figure, Geoffrey Grigson. As a charm against the angry melancholy which possessed him (and which made him so inclined, as reviewer or editor, to put the boot in), Grigson would often remind himself of Pasternak's maxim that 'we are the guests of existence' – hence the other face of his work, such invaluably loving and perceptive books as *The Englishman's Flora*, *The Private Art*, and the account of his Cornish homeground *Freedom of the Parish*. Would Sisson have scoffed at the maxim? Like these others, he was a man who had met a monster in his own mind, and remained permanently haunted by the meeting. What was this monster? Could he himself have said? I think of the reference in his essay 'Natural History' to 'an appalling adolescent grief' which struck him down – the moment when (he quotes the French novelist René Béhaine) he left behind him 'le sens du bonheur et le pouvoir d'être heureux'. I think of that enigmatic, unsatisfying sketch of a poem, 'The Mirabel Sea' ('There came a monster walking to me'); of 'Eastville Park' ('Wherever I went I came here first'); of 'Sea-fall':

Now if I am the enemy of myself
It is because love failed, my own.

*

I see now, as I did not for a long time after first reading him, that Sisson is shot through with contradictions; also that the contradictions are productive. Without them there would never have been the same imperious need to write. Some elements in this tangle I have already suggested. A full account of the contradictions would require an essay to itself, and would be political as well as personal in its explorations. I must content myself here by pointing to the most striking of them. Sisson is continually telling us, in his poems and elsewhere, that he lacks a sense of himself, that he is without individual identity. Often he goes on to suggest that if others feel differently about themselves, they are mistaken. Sometimes he seems to single himself out as a special case (already, with that 'himself' and 'special case', the contradiction suggests itself). Sometimes the difficulty is metaphysical, sometimes temperamental, sometimes a matter of class and education. But there is no question that the difficulty is tormentingly real for him. Yet it is Sisson, above all other poets, who insists both in his poetry and criticism that a poet stands or falls by the ability to discover and articulate a rhythm which is his or her own, an idiosyncrasy of voice which expresses a particular life and mind and view of things – as an artist's style is expressed, and the artist wholly present, even in the merest sketch. (I remember how he responded to and praised this quality in some Gaudier sketches in Kettle's Yard.) What Sisson points to here is what he seems simultaneously to deny – that elusive quality which makes a person himself or herself and no other; whatever it is which enables us to catch sight of someone (whom we may not have seen for years) crossing, in silhouette, the far end of a street down which we are walking, and to recognize them at once. It is this quality, carried into the language of poetry as its rhythm, which Sisson refers to in his Foreword to *In the Trojan Ditch* as 'that unarguable perception', and which his own poetry always sought out as its determining principle. For better or worse, and even in his adherence to a plain style, Sisson's poems – or a line or two from them – are instantly recognizable as his. Furthermore, if we read his work through, we end up knowing a great deal about him, and able to guess at more. Besides the poems and *On the Lookout*, there are the two autobiographical essays, 'Natural History' and the account he wrote for the Scribners *Contemporary Authors Autobiography Series* (Vol. 3) – which cannot be reprinted elsewhere for copyright reasons, but is worth seeking out as one of his best and most entertaining, as well as most revelatory prose writings. Yet all this from the man who tells us he isn't there! Is the poetry a way of finding out the missing existence, and giving it solidity; of bringing into the world the man who, as he tells us in 'Taxila', 'had not been born'? The contrast in his work between the distinct and the indeterminate, between the 'clear lake' and the 'new cloud', between the sharp appearances of the external world and the gloomy depth of the inward one, finds its emblem – trees standing out of mist – in another of my favourites among his poems, 'The Morning', which (so that I should have a poem by him in his own hand) I once asked him to write out for me:

I do not know what the mist signifies
When it comes, not swirling,
Gathering itself like briony under my window

The trees stand out of it,
Wading, you might say,
Have their dark tresses trailing in the water
Which began the world.

I can hear his voice as he would have said the poem – the throwaway 'you might say', the force of that transitive 'began' in the last line – the combined tentativeness and strength which help to make Sisson the poet he is.

John Peck

Charles Sisson and the Distantly Raised Voice

A reader hostile to Sisson's prevailing tone of self-erasure and melancholy might dismiss it as an echo of certain strains in early Eliot and Beckett. But such tone and sentiment are too native to Sisson to have been merely bolstered by the inventions of great precursors. Early and late he goes out in his own coat, to his own rhythms and on his own dour heading.

In theology, apophasis (literally the departure from what is shown or said; in speech an 'unsaying') is a way of going on gesturing anyhow toward the unsayable. Thus negative theology is a way of referring to the undiscussable, indeed unnameable nature and qualities of deity. Michael Sells spots the little turbine spinning within this paradoxical effort. 'The authentic subject of discourse slips continually back beyond each effort to name it or even to deny its nameability. The [linguistic] regress is harnessed and becomes the guiding semantic force, the *dynamis*, of a new kind of language'.[1] Such an engine, though its hum is discreet and though the subjects of poems are explicit, is electrically busy in much of Sisson's writing.

His focus for unsaying, early and late, is the flimsy of 'personality'. Only those who carry sturdy personal traits, a strong burden of 'I', know what it is to yearn for a vacation from them. Sisson's complaint carries the accents of a sensualist wearied by the inescapable sexual drive, but also of the individual who resists a pervasive, compliant submission to social conditioning. His satiric distancing from human behaviour, Swiftian with touches of Wyndham Lewis, is squeezed out like antibody against the conformities routinely induced by our shared context. His Old-Tory position of course formulates the necessary bulwarks, outer and inner, against these pressures. While he constantly professes a disdain toward the mystifications of 'I', those fashions in personality which compensate for conformity, his strength of feeling on these two scores—the impersonal inroads of lust, and the corrosive omnipresence of de facto collectivism—bespeak a sturdy sense of the person and its value (and thus personality and individuality in Jung's hard-won, unpopular sense, though Sisson had no truck with the Swiss doctor). One could not infer this from the manifest terms of the verse, which issues regular updates on skepticism about the existence of the subjective personality. A Buddhist teacher would hail this poet with a

---

[1] Michael Sells, *Mystical Languages of Unsaying*. University of Chicago Press, Chicago & London, 1994, 2.

'Well done!' But the *sous entendre* of the verse asserts that the soul of Mr Sisson remains in grave peril, assaulted continually in a desert where both Christian and older ways of supplying succour stay over the horizon. Dare I seriously maintain this about the editor of Anglican sermons? Yes, though only because certain evidence in the verse is there to be reckoned with. Its dryness, a dehiscence continually reiterated, testifies to surcease and relief only around twenty corners. Granted that that such agony is intrinsic to purification and spiritual ascesis, still, its tone in this honest body of work, an earnest self-communion with crumbling self, vitally whispers the lack of vitality. *Quo vadis?*

Sisson's self-disgust and his firm *contemptus mundi* meet up with belief that is equally firm, just as much pledged to biting honesty. For my money, the standoff between these two pressures shows up most clearly in a pair of adjacent poems in the *Collected Poems*, 'The Crucifix' and 'Trafalgar Square'. The first, in rhymed couplets, mounts paradoxes as keen as Donne's.

> O crucifix, you are indeed my lust,
>   You are the examination of my dust.
> My mind perjures and twists while you cry
>   Silently but so loud you tear the sky.
> Wherefore these tears? Shall I rejoice?
>   I would do, if I could hear your voice.[2]

Thus stands the counterpole to Sisson's celebrated challenge to Donne, to talk theology only after hauling out his genitals. That is, after such a seminar would come this narrower colloquy, where the *deus absconditus* is hidden in plain sight, and any shortfalls in sensing belong to consequent aspects of the I.

Yet even that does not go far enough. The previous collection (*Metamorphoses*, 1968) includes the great and corrosive litany 'Homo Sapiens is of No Importance', whose beginning summarizes the skeptical summa pieced out in 'Epictetus' or 'A Girl', in which an Epicurean ego (like a Buddhist one) hypothetically dissolves, and the grounds for theology with it.

> And it may be that we have no nature
> That he could have taken upon him.

---

[2] *Collected Poems*. Carcanet, Manchester, 1984, 178 (the new poems from *In the Trojan Ditch*).

In the rest of this short poem, which describes Jael's killing of Sisera, the tyrant's undoing becomes also an unsaying, for the eight phrases beginning 'Not for' turn out only glancingly, by implication, to acquire any single grammatical object:

> Not for the peg but for Sisera dead
> Not for Sisera dead but for his army routed
> Not for that but for the momentary ease under a tree
> Not for that but for the tree itself
> Not for the tree but for the sand blowing by it
> If there was any nature it was in that. [3]

This reduction of human nature *seriatim* inflects toward zero, as in a mock-Hasidic decreation, what Sisson's other searches and laments leave intact in their voicing. That is, in 'Homo Sapiens is of No Importance' the agonized believer allows his language to disintegrate around the long de-centering of the European ego by Copernicus, Darwin, and Freud. The length of that historical process reflects precisely the depth of tenacity with which the mind resists dispensing with the scaffolding of conventional identity. *Hic Rhodos* but usually *non salta*, yet this remarkable poem attempts that jump, vaulting slowly from 'may' to the driest of 'ifs' by way of apophatic litany.

The unreal aspects of personhood, then, affecting though they are, emerge from real afflictions to which the general would rather not own up.

> The poetry owners cannot make me out.

> Nor I them. And the big mouths of learning
> Open and close over my thoughts without biting.
> Under the shadow of politics I have no teeth.

> I am no man, Caesar, to stand by you,
> Nor have the whimsical humour of pre-war Oxford
> But my unrecognised style was made by sorrow.[4]

No matter what we make of this fellow, he will prove to be immensely valuable. For although sincere when he says that he is wretched, his wretchedness is the ground, not the ornament, of his manner.

---

[3] *Collected Poems*, 132.
[4] 'No Address', *Collected Poems*,173 (the same group from *In the Trojan Ditch*).

Sisson's fellow believers will defend him at this point, with some justice, as having maintained the posture of the sufferer who has found meaning in his suffering, sensualist though he may have been. They could cite his pained mood as exhibit A, in accord with Sylvanus of Athos, an early 20th-century monk, who was told by the inner Christ to 'Hold thy spirit in hell and do not despair, for in condemning himself to hell and in this destroying all passion, man liberates his heart to receive the divine love'.[5] Although this analogue closely beckons, it also misses by a mile the lament in Sisson's mood, which hardly bespeaks the resignation or stifled passion of the exemplar. Through the gap opened by that generous mile streams much of the verse.

From modern psychology, unfortunately, Sisson acknowledges only the Freudian direction, which he dispatches in a later poem from *Anchises* (1976), addressed to 'Marcus Aurelius'. My guess is that Sisson did not perceive the odd rightness of his wit at the expense of imperial egoism, a wit aimed at both the emperor and the doctor ('Old devil of Vienna, moving among the porcelain, / You were the beetle under the ruins of an empire'),[6] for it does not explicitly ironize Freud's reassertion of the I's centrality, in which wherever the unconscious was, ego shall be.

Although he does not lodge that note, taking aim only at the one-sidedly skeptical and by now journalistic notion titrated from Freud, Sisson's sense of the *individuum* remains entirely disillusioned. Nowhere in the new psychology did he find a notion of the person that would differently animate his Epictetean, skeptical critique of the I. My guess is that this was so because genuine mystery had gone into hiding—as it must for the Protestant mind of any stripe—and with it the chance for unbidden and overmastering original experience, which upends or blasts dryness with a wounding whose secret is renewal. In such an encounter, which brings direct knowledge rather than faith, the I, thoroughly relativized but newly necessary, can no longer remain the topic of lament.

To shift ground, and to conclude, I turn to the combined political-theological feeling that emerges from all of Sisson's effort. While this feeling is nothing that one can epitomize by way of single poems, its tenor rings most clearly, to my mind, in those few poems which unsay, indeed obliterate, certain grounds commonly held in our day.

My own non-Old-Tory experience persuades me that some of Sisson's political views, or for that matter some of Wyndham Lewis's, need not lead exclusively to the Old-Tory inferences and attitudes congenial to both men.

---

[5] As quoted by Thomas Merton in his journals for 4 September 1960: *Turning toward the World: The Pivotal Years,* ed. Victor A. Kramer. HarperSanFrancisco, HarperCollins, New York,1996, 42.
[6] *Collected Poems,* 223.

The distinction is a ticklish one to demonstrate, although some measure of its validity can be found in recent American decades, where a much younger system, lacking Britain's depth in time and traditions, nonetheless found thoughtful adherents on the libertarian Right and the constitutional Left parleying together against malignant tyranny. What makes for a lively mind in truly urgent political situations is not a *posse comitatus* of like views, but of unlike views converging upon limited, principled grounds. In adding poetry to this mix, I imagine a meeting of Heaney's Hamlet as spoken in 'Viking Dublin: Trial Pieces' with the dry declamation of Sisson's 'Anchises.' The first raises his voice loudly, advertising his slapdash vigor; the second restrains his utterance, pulling back, rather than pulling out, the stops which he carefully sounds through negation. The vigour arising from that meeting would not stem only from shared insights into corruption, or the weak leverage against it (a young man getting up his nerve, versus the shade of a dead man holding back from pronouncing auguries). It would also stem from the fact that opposed tones—bluster and dudgeon, over against fastidious disdain for assuming the guilt of empire—register kindred ironies.

I am Hamlet the Dane,
skull-handler, parablist,
smeller of rot

in the state, infused
with its poisons,
pinioned by ghosts
and affections,

murders and pieties,
coming to consciousness
by jumping in graves,
dithering, blathering.[7]

*

This is my proper sightlessness,
The invisible pack hunting the visible air.
There are those who exist, but it is not I.

[7] Seamus Heaney, *North*. Faber, London, 1975, 23.

32

Existent are: bodies, although their existence is
Not proven; tremors
Through the vast air expecting some other thing
Not known, or hopeless; or else hoped for and lost.
One could devise invisibility,
Walking by it as if it were not obligatory
As it is with me, *moi qui n'existe pas*
NON SUM, therefore NON COGITO, although there are shapes
Upon a mind I sometimes take to be mine.
This is not much to show for sixty years
Here by the Latin gate, or where the Baltic
Spreads its white arms over the barren sand.
Do not number me on this seashore
Where the effete light from the north
Floods over the ice-cap. I came from Troy
It was not after she had ended, but before.[8]

Heaney's ironizing on widely shared inefficacies touches back to that talismanic, cornered strategist who famously feigns effeteness in order to gain his tactical chance. A murdered patrimony, a felled father, disposes the fate which raises that voice—to an unsteady altitude, where bluster rehearses vengeance but grasps after its opening. How suitably that often characterizes what shadows the lofty pitch of progressives in the modern West! And therefore, to avoid what Heaney calls its blather, George Oppen, most notably, chose never to raise his voice. The finest, strongest register of the old communist, renegade rich-man's son, and community organizer is noble without a trace of push. Sisson's poem—which achieves the summa of his skeptical posture, the codex of his chief stance, more so even than in 'The Usk'—speaks from the core of Western patrimony, it seems, in the arch-father's voice. But not really, for it comes from a spirit self-maintained since *before* Troy's fall and its fateful assimilation to Rome. This father utters no prophecies useful to the programme of imperial legend.

To point the comparison more succinctly: the raised voice gets raised, at least at first, ineffectually, whereas the distantly raised voice already assumes a negative wisdom, choosing irony over engagement. One might call its gambit the higher ineffectuality, although Sisson's dry litany of disclaimers quietly affirms, with its parting Trojan shot, that its stuff is steel, however insubstantial it may seem to moderns. Both voices know what it is to carry the burden of personality, and therefore tactically to feign either a mad lack

---

[8] *Collected Poems*, 236-237.

33

of access to effective means, or explicitly to desist from them and all their categories, even thought and body.

I mention Oppen alongside Sisson, of course, exclusively on the basis of tone. Oppen nowhere takes refuge in historical irony, and he is Sisson's political and temperamental counterpart. Yet politics, from the standpoint of the soul's longer views, rings notoriously hollow—that is, the spirit at which one hammers away in one's privacy is itself the most considerable offering any of us makes to, or the actual impact any of us finally has upon, what we call history. And that effect, equally notoriously, remains largely or even entirely invisible to us: it seems to count for nothing in the terms allowed by the main drift of opinion and the various shades of partisan urgency. In that respect, 'Anchises' indeed utters a prophecy, but an apophatic one, whose negations articulate a spiritual realism of drastically reduced means in modern mass conditions. Spiritual hygiene in this respect goes hand in hand with Sisson's instinctive aversion to the main, Left ideological line-ups of his formative decade. His essays on both matters, overall, converge on the sense that acumen in one realm will clarify matters in the other. His 'Autobiographical Reflections on Politics' of 1954 keenly trace the development of the inferences to which his pre-war travel in Europe led him, in ways that illuminate unities of feeling throughout the verse. The fact that for him recent French political theory and history led him back to the English 17th century for his definitive sorting-out is germane to his skepticism, toward not only solutions on the Left but also his sometime-guide Maurras, who became 'confused and confusing'.[9]

I single out that essay, uncollected until 1978 in *The Avoidance of Literature*, because in its workings I find the basis for Sisson's praise of the 'naturalness in the way of thinking' which he found in Herbert, Vaughan, and Traherne, long before encountering Eliot (as he avowed to Clive Wilmer in interview).[10] That thinking takes up both the organic nature of the realm, that is, the actually lived customs of political community, and then the mind that goes down simultaneously into sensual life and out into the soil of faith. Sisson's great argument is that this mind is of necessity a national mind, with a history that will out in the sane individual, dour though its current run may be. His insistence on the privacy of the drama, however—its cussedly anarchic focus in thought alongside loyalty to the soil of fact and belief—makes this drama the Late Protestant one. The kind of history that we actually make within

---

[9] *The Avoidance of Literature: Collected Essays*, ed. Michael Schmidt. Carcanet, Manchester, 1978, 143.
[10] Clive Wilmer, ed., *Poets Talking: The 'Poet of the Month' interviews from BBC Radio 3*. Carcanet, Manchester, 1994, 10.

its skeptic walls may either console us or drive us wild, depending on our mood. Consolation, however, is on very short offer in Sisson's world, which is the world of most western people since the Reformation. In that world genuine mystery, though it still may be persistently desired, has evaporated. The dryness in Sisson's skeptical tone therefore runs alongside a matching dehiscence in Protestant feeling. Not by jumping into graves does it come to consciousness, but by living in a grave quietly with the *deus absconditus*, on terms of loyalty with the enclosing walls of inherited earth. Evangelical élan finds its own stairway out of this, but on terms that nowhere touch this other, radically stoic attitude. Only the soul's appetite for mystery, which in these conditions is both sharply and heavily felt, utters just Sisson's kind of persistent self-deflation and self-negation, so as to remain up to both its desire and the actual conditions.

By that very token, 'Anchises', along with its cousin 'Homo Sapiens is of No Importance', lends scope and distance to Sisson's most persistent spirit, his unsaying of personhood and its meaning in our conditions. The midrash on Sisera's death at the hands of Jael builds the platform, as it were, for the second poem's folding of Sisson's anthropology into the shared life of history. The invention of a pre-Roman voice for Anchises—as if Tate's kindred 'Aeneas at Washington' were to manifest as a Beckett monad—raises the pitch of Sissonian skepsis and its lament, by virtue of assigning it to remote eminence, on a barren height that reverses the Virgilian current by gainsaying effectuality.

Therefore the proper backdrop for Sisson's Anchises is not the later speeches by that figure in Sisson's own translation of *Aeneid* 5 and 6, but the dehiscent litany spoken near Sisera's tent in 'Homo Sapiens'. These two poems by Sisson inscribe the spare, titanium arc which Sisson threw over his skeptical tone—elevated at great distance, and resonant in the hollowed-out majesty of self-erasure. In raising that arc of minimalist passion, they mark a characteristic limit of poetic definition in this writer: clearly at the back wall, rather than out in the middle among the modernist shadings of 'In insula Avalonia' and 'The Usk', which as Sisson remarked to Clive Wilmer 'represent an attempt to be plain about a state of mental confusion.'[11] In the Sisera-Anchises pair, where he devolved definition to degree zero by combining unsaying with negative expansion, he found amplitude for his most persistent attitude—and for some large quotient, therefore, of the actual effect he has had on our shared life as an earnest private speaker, rather than as an eminent authority on public administration. The distant

[11] Ibid., 9-10.

elevation of this voice could thereby attain the dignity of a *before*, and of a desert elsewhere, which stepped around the nostalgia that sometimes rings from poetic modernism. Protestant and Old Tory, but apophatic as well, this spirit, claiming that it hailed from a pre-Romantic deme, survives in current conditions only by continually moulting and stripping. The 'naturalness in the way of thinking' which Sisson heard in the Christian poets of the 17th century, he heard also with ears perpetually rinsed of illusions. And that tension in the ear, steely and adamant along its further reaches, rings true. Thus the asperity in these two poems carries a distinctive kind of grandeur. In them one hears an earnest, persistent self-undoing, mordantly overheard by someone compelled to unsay a great deal, greatly.

Michael Schmidt

C. H. Sisson and his Editor

What did I say in all that ink
I spilt in poems, in novels or
The prose in which men say they think?
What was all that effusion for?

Christopher Ricks, interviewed some years ago about Donald Davie, reflected on how hard it is to speak of 'those of whom one is oneself made'. When I started writing a book on ancient Greek poetry, Freddie Raphael warned me it would be difficult to get a purchase on them because 'they are what we know'. For me Charles Sisson was a formative – *the* formative – figure in my early adult life. He was there shortly after the birth of Carcanet, he attended at the birth of *PN Review*, and at a personal level he and Nora were godparents to my first son, Charles.

Writing about him entails bringing into conscious focus elements which are part of my second nature; the focus is tentative and any conclusions are provisional and personal. I knew Charles for more than three decades, visited him in London and then in Langport, perhaps thirty or forty times over the years. He and Nora came to stay in Manchester. My first substantial achievement as an editor, in my view, was the recovery and publication of the first thirty-odd years of his writing. He spoke plain, but in many different registers and forms. I was never sure I understood; and despite the profound underlying themes, in particular the theme of England, there is something exasperatingly provisional when one considers his readjustment to a receding tide, his acquisition and then his loss of faith, his harsh and demanding hope and its expiry.

Change can be traced in his poetic styles, his translations, and his prose writings. What retains its fascination is the trajectory, rich in durable milestones but with no prolonged or conclusive destination. Many of the writers he most admired, from Andrew Marvell to Wyndham Lewis, John Donne to Ford Madox Ford, were like him on a journey, their best work marking vivid points along the way.

*

Hard to say: if it has a meaning
The words are there, you can find out

And you will find the author leaning
To too much hope or too much doubt

At Robert Nye's suggestion, C. H. Sisson submitted his poetry to Carcanet when he was in his late fifties. I did not like the work he sent: I could not 'hear' it. But I asked to see his earlier poems, and it was while reading *Metamorphoses* (1968) and in particular the title sequence, that I heard him plain. Those curious unrhymed couplets have the tact and efficiency of rhyme, and a rare Marvellian suppleness. The economy and transparency of the images (especially in the Europa passage that concludes part IV), and the electrifying Nativity and Easter 'metamorphosis of all' (part IX), persuaded me that he was a major poet. From there I read forward to the newer poems, then back to *Numbers*. I had found my way into the poetry. Gradually I got to know the man, as much as he was to be known by someone so remote from him in antecedent and culture. In my case it was a matter of filial adoption: I revered, resisted and honoured him. I still do.

Carcanet published his first collected poems and selected translations, *In the Trojan Ditch* (1974), commissioned his translations, resurrected his novels, and I edited a vast corpus of four decades of his essays in *The Avoidance of Literature* (1978), a book whose 580 pages I typeset on an old IBM golf-ball composing machine. I proofread and indexed it too. It ran to something over a quarter of a million words. Preparing the book, which starts with the *New English Weekly* pieces from 1937 (he was then the age of his new editor) and ends with essays and editorials composed for *PN Review* in 1977 (he was then roughly the age I am now), took us three years, the same time my undergraduate degree had taken. Having read his essays, I followed up on many of their subjects, acquiring Filmer and Hooker, Ford and Lewis (both of whom I came to publish), Pound (at last I got into Pound), the Vaughans, Clarendon (his and Nora's wedding gift was a handsome edition of *The History of the Rebellion*), T. E. Hulme, MacDiarmid, Swift, Jeremy Taylor, William Barnes and others. Among his contemporaries I was soon reading and publishing David Wright, Cliff Ashby, W. S. Graham, George Barker, John Heath-Stubbs. I turned to him for advice on books to be translated, so that Botho Strauss, Abdelhak Serhane, Jean-Louis Baghio'o and others were published thanks to his advocacy.

Though we continued to collaborate creatively and editorially until his health failed – another two decades – I was closest to his writings in 1978 when I had published *In the Trojan Ditch* and the compendious book of essays. The development of his work that I had traced, issuing the poems in reverse chronology and the essays in a more or less forward chronology, surprised me. The chief consistency was in tone. Revisiting the work today, I am still moved by its range and by the ways in which connections and tensions exist at every point. I am still most at home with his work from the late 1960s and the 1970s, though his final sequence, 'Tristia', burns to the very quick.

*

– Sometimes, they say, to plain despair;
More often, I would say, observing,
Quite simply, certain things are there
And that is more or less deserving
As others think they are there too

I find it difficult to write about Charles Sisson in terms appropriate for this celebration. I have written about him a dozen times. This is not a place for exposition but for another kind of response. Personal? As with an absent parent, I conduct continual discussions, arguments and reconciliations with him.

In a wry, tenacious spirit, he never let me forget the fact that I was not British except by adoption ('a benighted Mexican' he called me – and perhaps the depth and integrity of his embodied Englishness is what attracted me to him most, even as it repels some of his fellow countrymen). There were things I would never understand, it was clear, try as I might: crucial elements in a rooted culture are given and cannot be acquired by someone with the keenness of a convert. He found Eliot's Englishness constructed and often suspect: the wrong karma, perhaps, the wrong choices, wrong because choices. Now that his culture seems less rooted even than it did in the 1970s, the attraction of his perspectives becomes even stronger. I remember writing to George Steiner that I was trying to put down roots in a Sissonian England. He said that he was a Jew and had learned not to put down roots but to use his legs. In time, I have become more realistic, I suppose, more of a Jew than I was, yet there is still a longing for roots of the kind that nourished C. H. Sisson's imagination, and nostalgia for the years in which I believed such roots might be acquired.

There it is again, beneath that longing for stability the recurrent fact of process and change, in the writer, in the environment at large; it weighed on him historically and vocationally. I do not like to use the term 'development' which suggests intention and direction, and in some respects the poetry which strikes me as most complex and achieved is that from the late 1960s and early 1970s, the most compelling essays from the 1950s and 1960s. In the thirty years of our friendship, he moved and moved rapidly; I was at best several steps behind him; and often I did not anticipate or understand what caused his

changes or the directions in which they led. For repose I returned to the ways
he had gone, the works I already knew best.

*

– And that includes the dead, as well
As critics A and B, or you,
And how right you are, time will tell.

I'd like to offer a few memories of the writer, speaking as his publisher
and a reader who loves some of his poems and essays more than those of
any other contemporary, though that love can be vexed and disappointed by
the reconfigurations in the writer which demanded change in the committed
reader too.

The most acute change I had to adjust to was his reluctant yet in retrospect
inevitable falling away from the Church of England. I had become a
communicant Anglican again in the wake of reading his essays and the
Anglican divines about whom he wrote. I was moved by the severity and
the rigorous unsentimentality of his account of the Church in its most
contentious and articulate period. Without him the Anglican Classics series in
our Fyfield*Books* list (Hooker, Law, Latimer, Taylor, the Anglican Newman
and others) would not have been launched, or the vast three-volume set of
The English Sermon, for which he edited the second volume and wrote the
introductions for the first, under the general editorship of his friend Martin
Seymour-Smith.

His spiritual trajectory affected me, as it did other readers – and how could it
not have done? He came to speak to my students at the University of Manchester
late in the 1970s. After he read, a student suggested that his religious views
were a matter of opinion, like any other. He struck the board: they are, for
a believer, he declared, a matter of truth. The spiritual and imaginative
movement whose beginnings occasion the poem 'In Memoriam Cecil de Vall:
late garrison chaplain, Barrackpore' ('I have resigned the pretensions/Of the
individual will') here reached a climax of unambiguous affirmation. But his
experience was to prove not unlike that of Henry Vaughan, whom he evokes
in his eloquent essay 'Songs in the Night' (1973). 'Where is God my Maker,
who giveth Songs in the night?' Job asked, and Vaughan asked on the title
page of *Silex Scintillans*, and Sisson asks in his essay, 'telling the truth, and
having some truth to tell'. The truths the later poems tell are of a different
order from the truths of the poems Sisson published in the late 1960s and for
the decade or so after.

I asked Charles to translate *The Divine Comedy* in 1973 because the poem

40

of his I loved best then, and now, is 'In insula Avalonia'. On one visit to Langport we drove out and he pointed to 'this large oak/Which stands with all its leaves throughout the year', in the middle of a field. It was in part III of 'In insula'. Every natural detail of that astonishing poem answers to the literal Somerset landscape, the lived space which he and generations before him had experienced, while at the same time the poem explored an historical and a transcendent dimension. The prosody struck me as Dantesque, versatile and flexible in its basic three-line stanza structure; the poem's particularism, too, was in tune with the Italian original, where the literal and the allegorical inhabit the same details. Though he had fished successfully in other men's waters before, in Heine's and Ovid's, Virgil's and Horace's, he resisted Dante, preferring to tackle Horace's *Ars Poetica* which in a Poundian spirit he brought into the present world; and Lucretius's *De Rerum*. That translation relates deeply to the poems he was writing at the time and to the thematic transformation that was to occur.

By the time he wrote to say he was ready to undertake Dante, what had seemed the ideal moment had passed. The imagination that produced the sounds and sense of 'In insula' had moved on. In the 'Foreword' to *In the Trojan Ditch* he wrote, 'as the inevitable facility comes, the conscious task becomes the rejection of whatever appears with the face of familiarity'. There was no question, on this fishing expedition, of his recreating deliberately sounds and strategies appropriate to an earlier expedition. He was a different poet now. He insists, 'The proof of the poem – any poem – is in its rhythm and that is why critical determination has in the end to await that unarguable perception.' His Dante remains unproven, to my hearing; it is ironic that of all his translations it is this one that has travelled furthest in the world. Apart from the *Paradiso* with its 'pin ball lights', which come alive and illuminate the poems he was writing at the time, there is a pedestrian quality: not the rhythms of speech but half way between speech and prose, the literal sense dragging like a broken wing and Dante's form reflected only in the stanza breaks. Just occasionally it flutters into the air, but falls back to the sulphurous pathway again, and hops along.

Had he worked on the translation before his retirement to Langport, it would have been a different kind of engagement and creation, a product of the stolen hours that brought forth the Heine as he set off, a young soldier sailing to India in 1943; and the Catullus and Virgil's *Eclogues* while he was commuting to his Civil Service job in London, each accomplished in a different way in moments wrested from a life of activity, each relating closely to the poems he was writing at the time. The Dante began too late; the translation came too easily, without the transformative qualities that mark the rapt prosody of 'In insula'.

41

I typeset many of Charles's early Carcanet books right up to 1980. And when I was typesetting the Lucretius and Virgil's *Aeneid* I had to punctuate. Charles's firm belief in the power and sufficiency of achieved rhythm meant that for him the issue of 'correct' punctuation did not arise. For his editor it very much did: the punctuation needed to be consistent and correct. The theme bored the poet. I punctuated as I typeset, submitted the proofs to him, and he did not recoil. He was not a natural proof reader: having written the poem, essay or translation, his work was done, and he missed most of the errors; but he also overlooked the quite extensive drizzle of punctuation that fell on his translations. And he did not revise much at proof stage: the work was abandoned by the time it went to press, the process of writing was over, and the process of publishing had begun. In his acceptance of editorial punctuation and the formal adjustments of the publishing process I sensed his realism at work: the battles worth fighting did not for him generally entail a comma, a semicolon or a full stop. They might entail a line or a stanza, though even here he welcomed editing, whether from David Wright, his chief quality controller, or from me. If he resisted it was because the poem was right as it stood.

We never had battles, though we disagreed fundamentally on certain subjects. American poetry was one. He insisted on juxtaposing Christina Rossetti and Emily Dickinson, always to Dickinson's disadvantage; he was mildly affronted when I compared the prosodic qualities of 'In insula' to those of some of my favourite Wallace Stevens poems. He had little time – he had no time – for Stevens. Within the Carcanet list there were authors whose work we tactfully left out of our conversations, in particular John Ashbery. Yet he had written long before I met him about Edgell Rickword and Hugh MacDiarmid. His sympathy with the radical voices in the tradition was profound; he was also inclined to be patient with the poetry and fiction of Laura Riding.

Charles and I exchanged letters every week, sometimes every day, for many years. His correspondence with me now lives at the John Rylands University of Manchester Library, and I hope one day a book of these letters, and his correspondence with David Wright and other poets will be published. W.S. Graham admired his work and once sent him a Roger Hilton pastel in appreciation (I imagine Charles may have sent him the occasional gift of money because he was aware of the Grahams' circumstances).

His collection of paintings and sculptures was another aspect of his life story, changing tastes, changing images, and evidence of a modernist spirit. Apart from the intense pleasure his own work provides, C.H. Sisson's writings take the unbiased reader into areas of the Anglo-American and European Modern which are out of favour and out of fashion now but which are, as his work is, crucial to any serious future that British, and specifically English, art will have.

Clive Wilmer

C.H. Sisson in Place: The 'Garden' Poems and the English Church

I remember recommending Charles Sisson's poetry, more than twenty years ago, to my friend the American poet Edgar Bowers. 'Sisson?' he queried, with a note of mischief in his voice, 'Isn't he the Anglican who isn't a Christian?' There's many a true word spoken in jest, and it must be admitted that Bowers had a point. Donald Davie, second to none in his admiration of Sisson, told me how shocked he had been when Sisson declared he could never have been a Christian without being an Anglican. This is not identical to Bowers's caricature, but it surely echoes it, and we should not forget that Charles Maurras, one of the young Sisson's crucial heroes, was a Roman Catholic who didn't believe in God. Maurras would probably have preferred the Roman Church to worship Roman gods, but history having imposed the God of the Jews, the function of that Latin institution was to discipline and contain the Semitic spirit. At any rate, the choice of religion, for Maurras, was mainly to do with nationalism and the seats of power. Close as Sisson's position was to his, I think the two must be carefully distinguished. Richard Hooker, in Sisson's words, was 'the classic apologist of *the* Church of *England*: not a sect, but the historic heir of the medieval church; not a world-wide federation of theological opinion, like contemporary Anglicanism, but the one Sun seen, as it were, through the mists of this island – the only way it can in truth be seen, from this perspective.'[1] This is, in George Orwell's terms, patriotism rather than nationalism: more an expression of love than one of power, though a loved place – as Sisson was well aware – needs political power to defend and sustain it. More importantly, though, the quotation implies that the believer has no option: that seekers after absolute truth must settle for the restricted views their circumstances offer.

The argument is addressed with still more passion in an essay on Coleridge's *Church and State*, which first appeared in 1977, some years before the Hooker piece. Here Sisson expresses a preference for those who are 'content to be merely the Church *in a place*' [my italics], as against those in favour of that 'world-wide federation of opinion'. He prefers them because, 'faced with the unintelligibility of the language the church speaks, I am of a religion in which – to adapt Coleridge's phrase – Christianity is an accident; the religion

---

[1] 'Richard Hooker and the *Ecclesiastical Polity*', *Is There a Church of England?* (Manchester: Carcanet, 1993), p. 210. First published in *The Salisbury Review* (Winter, 1983).

of our fathers, or the *mère patrie*, of the spirits buried in the ground, of the religion of England, I cannot help it.'[2] An admirer of Sisson's, the art critic Tom Lubbock, has remarked of this that 'Coleridge's phrase is "a blessed accident", but he hastens to assure the reader that he means a Godsend. As Sisson adapts it, it sounds more like a mere circumstance': which is surely to suggest that, far from being a Christian, Sisson believes in a universe governed by chance, though occupied by tutelary spirits.[3]

In any event, it is hardly surprising that as he grew older, and as the Church of opinion – in particular of opinions locked in conflict – grew more and more prominent, Sisson found less and less room for himself in what he had long thought his natural home. The essay on Hooker dates from 1983. About four years before that date, he had more or less given up going to church.

What happens to a person who believes in a truth which for him finds expression in a particular institution, when that institution ceases to exist? For the true particularist there can be no alternative. Yet surely a belief, once as securely lodged in Sisson's consciousness as in the Church itself, could not simply have disappeared. That is to say, could Sisson, through ceasing to be an Anglican, have become an atheist? Strange though it may seem, that is a real possibility, since it was only the English Church that preserved Sisson from the full implications of a pessimism – especially a pessimism about human nature – that verged on nihilism. The world of his novel *Christopher Homm*, for instance, is that of human life untouched by Grace: a life every bit as bleak as that we are shown in the plays of Samuel Beckett or the paintings of Francis Bacon. Moreover, Sisson's literary passions had always included works by rigorous materialists – Lucretius, for instance, whom he memorably translated. Neither materialism nor atheism was wholly foreign to his way of thinking. So when the vehicle for his religious convictions died, what of the sacred was left to occupy his consciousness?

The answer to that question ought to be easy, for Sisson was a prolific poet and the matter of his soul was to a large extent the matter of his poetry. Yet it is not at all clear. The first collection he published after leaving the Church was *Exactions* (1980), which includes what is for me the finest sheaf of poems in his *oeuvre*: the 'garden' poems, most of them reflections on his terraced garden at Langport with its heartbreakingly beautiful view of the plain bisected by the River Parrett and focused by the tower of Muchelney Church. These poems set out from a sense of emptiness at the heart of the individual – the absence of anything one could call the self – and reach out towards the material world

[2] 'Coleridge Revisited', *Is There a Church of England?* p. 129. First published in *PN Review*, 5.1 (1977).

[3] Tom Lubbock, 'One for All and All for One', *Independent on Sunday*, 8 August 1993, p. 18.

of growth and decay. Not the world in general, but a particular place: a garden
and, beyond it, a landscape, and all that follows from that:

> There is not Nothing if not I
> For 'I' is only emptiness.
> And what comes flooding in? The Time,
> The Place: the Matter, nothing less.
>
> ('The Matter')

The Matter, I take it, is both the great subject – as in 'the Matter of Britain'
– and mere material things: those things that are indubitably existent, unlike
certain spiritual conceptions. If God is there, it is as a linguistic usage:

> A man is like a plant, he has to grow
> And then to die. Not always in one place,
> Yet he is rooted. What does the stem encase?
> Nothing that did not come from the root or the air,
> Which is full of voices; nothing which does not go
> To the shrivelled heap and the Lord have mercy on it.
>
> ('The Plant')

The emphasis on 'nothing' in both these short poems seems paradoxically
to affirm everything – everything except the human individual. One must
emphasise 'individual', for the place is also 'full of voices', which are oddly
more substantial than any physical presence: the voices, for instance, of
legendary figures from Malory '[a]nd the battle-pile of those he accounted
dead'. The poem I refer to there, the marvellous 'In Flood', is the poem
most evocative of the world beyond the garden – Somerset, the ground
and constitution of England and the immaterial England of her language
and literature, as embodied in the *Morte Darthur*. The flooded plain which
provokes these meditations gives surprising substance to the 'flooding in'
of time and place in 'The Matter', an image that might otherwise seem
a cliché. The Sisson of 'In Flood' looks forward to becoming one of the
dead, with the further paradox or contradiction that he himself will be
'speechless' among the voices:

> Only glad that when I go to join them
> I shall be speechless, no one will ask my name,
> Yet among the named dead I shall be gathered,
> Speaking to no man, not spoken to, but in place.

That final phrase cannot but recall 'the Church in a place' from 'Coleridge Revisited', though now the church is no more than a physical building, like the tower of the parish church he no longer attended looking over the garden-wall in the closing lyric of 'Burrington Combe'. In that poem we also hear how

> No distance was ever like this one
> The flat land with its willows, and the great sky
> With the river reflecting its uncertainty
> But no more I

– that final line the complement to 'in place'.

It might be argued that, riven as it is with contradiction, the intellectual position is hardly logical. Sisson retains his scorn of sinful humanity, which now has nothing to redeem it but the physical graces of loved natural things and echoes of the dead in the words they once uttered. It might be urged that there can be no language without humanity and that human beings cannot be so contemptible if they have been able to create such an artefact. In a Christian dispensation, the achievement of a common human speech can be attributed to the Logos, the incarnate Word of St John's Gospel; without a Church to gather our attempts at speech together, our language can be no more than a collection of separate and fragmentary utterances. What this inconsistency seems to suggest is that Sisson in his last years had to live with a contradiction: with the God he had long believed in but no Church through which to speak to him and of him.

The effect of this was partly to intensify Sisson's particularism. Where previously he had talked of the truth as mediated by specific and local conditions, he was now preoccupied with the conditions alone. He had always been impatient with large abstractions and generalities. He now became unwilling to talk about general truths at all, except as the consequences of empirical observations. I remember a conversation in which I referred to 'The Red Admiral' – perhaps my favourite of the garden poems – as a poem about death. He replied with some asperity, 'I rather thought it was about a butterfly.' I saw, and see, the objection – the poem is a meditation on a specific object in particular circumstances – but his position does give rise to intellectual difficulties. The poem is undoubtedly about an insect, which is beautifully observed, but it also gives rise to several human concerns, most of them with general implications:

The old light fades upon the old stones;
The day is old: how is there such light
From grey clouds? It is the autumnal equinox,
And we shall all have shrunk before daylight.

The setting is both literally and figuratively autumnal, and much the same can be said for the twilight hour: 'The mystery is only the close of day'. Memory crowds out

what cannot be remembered;
Better to have none, best of all when
The evening sunlight has ended.

It is hard not to think of autumn, the ageing year, the shrinking, the close of day, the sunset and the forgetfulness as images of old age and approaching death. But in doing so, we generalise a particular experience, as we always do when we meditate or philosophise – indeed, whenever we convert experience into language. 'The Red Admiral' is resistant to that process – resistant to it even as it engages in it. This is most strikingly the case in the final stanza:

Its fingers lighter than spiders, the red admiral
Considers, as I do, with little movement;
With little of anything that is meant:
But let the meaning go, movement is all.

To 'let the meaning go' is to abandon hope of glimpsing 'the one Sun' – and one must wonder whether a sun that cannot be perceived can be thought to exist at all. On the other hand, the loss of a truth refracted through particulars may encourage a deeper devotion to the particulars, now somehow rendered empty of significance. Sisson clearly conceives of the butterfly, sufficiently absorbing in itself, as the antithesis of an emblem – as having no significance beyond itself – though paradoxically it thus becomes the emblem of an absence. What that absence is – whether it amounts to the absence of God, or merely the absence of a context in which to speak to God – we are not told, and probably cannot know.

Timothy Harris

But let the meaning go...

I first came across C.H. Sisson's poetry and essays years ago, when I was still fairly young, in the pages of *PN Review*. I liked the poetry and respected the essays, and sent him a letter, together with some bad poems of my own, in which I wrote that I admired his poetry while disagreeing with his politics (I was and remain a social democrat in the Karl Polanyi mould). I think that he was amused by this, and he wrote a kind letter back in which, among other things, he gave me an introduction to Michael Schmidt at *PN Review*. Subsequently, I visited Charles and Nora at Langport on two occasions, when I happened to be in England (for I have lived for thirty-five years in Japan). Sisson was a shy, gentle and immensely kind man, with an acute intelligence, and a fine, anarchic sense of mischief – a sense that was connected, I think, with his sense of the teeming formlessness of the self ('Yet it is she who has become definite; / I never did.'). These qualities all inform what might seem to be the severe and forbidding *persona* that performed the wittily cruel dissection of George Steiner's *On Difficulty* in the *TLS* back in 1978 (I have kept it for thirty years) and that is presented in the poems:

> But my heart is armoured by intellection;
> My heart has been hardened:
> On that account I catch my trains with precision
> And know how to look after myself, mate.

The poem from which those lines are quoted, 'The Adventurer', might be classified as an epigram, and its sharp, spare style goes back through Pound, Swift and Jonson to the Latin epigrammatists, though the self-deprecation and savage humour are very much Sisson's own (nobody, so far as I know, has remarked on how genuinely comic a poet he can be: a great many of the poems are extremely funny). But there is much more to the poetry than a style given over to surfaces, armoured by intellection and possessing a directness and energy of utterance. Writing of the *Pisan Cantos* in a perceptive essay on Pound, Sisson quotes some beautifully wondering lines about lynxes, pards and bassarids, and writes, 'We are in the depths of the poet's mind, and what should one find in such a situation except images?' And what characterises Sisson's poetry, it seems to me, is a tension between the superficies of language, which is 'all our lies' and 'has us on a skewer', and the wordless depths and dissolutions beneath it: sleep 'Knows us for plants or undiscovered

48

worlds; / If we have reasons, they lie deep'. There is a tension, too, between spontaneous tenderness and the cold and unbearable lessons provided by the world as well as by Christianity:

I almost prayed for its departing
The tiny bird with sodden feathers
The Christian faith forbids such pity

('A Duckling')

Sisson was at times perhaps too ready to accept such cold lessons (to my agnostic mind, a faith that forbids pity in the case of a dying duckling deserves at least a little questioning), but in general the cold lessons he learned from such as Charles Maurras and Georges Sorel he applied in a very intelligent and humane way. He was no respecter of violence, but he recognised clearly the part it plays in human affairs and rightly had no truck with the sort of disingenuous or cynical moralising that led Tony Blair to join George Bush's invasion of Iraq and leads him to continue to justify his disastrous decision and to prettify horror and suffering. The essays collected in the various volumes published by Carcanet, notably *The Avoidance of Literature*, provide an illuminating perspective on the world and on writers, and, in the rigour and honesty of their analyses, provide also a corrective to the abstractions, both of the left and the right, that so rule our public discourse, our criticism and our minds. I say 'both of the left and the right', since it does not seem to me to be helpful to think of Sisson, as he is commonly thought of, as a man of the 'right'. Although a lover of England (*'O gentile Engleterre, a toi j'escrits'*) and a patriot, he was in no way a chauvinist, and there is in fact quite a bit of common ground between him and such thinkers of the 'left' as the sociologist Pierre Bourdieu and the economist Amartya Sen, both of whom are as opposed to destructive abstractions as he was.

The Avoidance of Literature: the title itself, for me, was wonderful. Partly, perhaps, because I had not enjoyed school much, had read voraciously on my own and had not gone on to university, I had always disliked the idea of 'Literature' as an object of academic study, and such ideas as the 'Western canon' or the various 'canons' of English literature espoused by such critics as F. R. Leavis or Harold Bloom. One reads books for enjoyment and stimulation. There was no such thing as a 'canon', it seemed to me, but rather a tradition, whose contours changed with one's changing interests and which had all sorts of interesting byways for exploration (W. H. Hudson, Izaak Walton, John Bunyan, Thomas Middleton, James Hogg, John Clare), some of whom, like Middleton and Clare, were great neglected writers or, like Hogg, the author of at least one indisputably great work – *The Confessions of a Justified Sinner*. Another reason for thinking in terms of a tradition, rather than a canon existing in some purely aesthetic, literary, or educational space and consisting only of poems, plays and novels, with perhaps a couple of collections of essays thrown in, is that it allows us to refer readily to, say, the sermons of Lancelot Andrewes or William Law's *A Serious Call to a Devout and Holy Life* (Sisson recommends Law's prose as some of the liveliest of his century), and – to turn away from religion – to works such as Bacon's Essays, G. H. Hardy's *A Mathematician's Apology* and Richard Dawkins' excellent writings on evolution. By avoiding 'Literature', Sisson's approach allows letters to be seen to play a very real part in life, and not merely in our private lives. It opens things up, and allows us a fuller and richer view.

I also disliked the habit, common among critics (Bloom, for example), of weighing, say, Shakespeare and Marlowe, or Shakespeare and Jonson, or Shakespeare and Milton, with the balance usually being brought down on the side of Shakespeare: one admires different writers for different reasons, and though contemporaries as well as generations have their rivalries, as well as disagreements, sometimes profound, that still reverberate today and require recognition, they are not necessarily entered in some eternal competition. So that one very attractive aspect of Sisson's essays was his refusal to take sides in the quarrel that is supposed to exist between avowedly modernist writers like Pound and other modern writers like Edward Thomas, a quarrel for which the modernists and their supporters, with their anathemas and deprecations, bear a not inconsiderable responsibility – a fact that makes me sympathise strongly with Philip Larkin's passionate defence of Thomas Hardy, though I have small time for the vulgarity of his dismissal of modernism, just as I have small time for the vulgarity of his politics, which was little more than a sort of posturing designed to win plaudits from the similarly prejudiced and to annoy those whose ideas and prejudices he disliked.

Sisson's criticism and political writings are in almost no way posturing or prejudiced, except (where prejudice is concerned) in E. M. Cioran's sense, mentioned with approval by Sisson in *Anglican Essays*, of prejudices as organic truths, false in themselves, but 'accumulated through generations and transmitted' and with whose 'duration and consistency' the duration and consistency of a collectivity, such as a tribe or a nation, coincides. He thinks deeply and is mostly very fair-minded (I say 'mostly' because his remarks on Ireland in the autobiographical *On the Look-out*, although in some respects not unjustified, are couched in such terms as are bound to cause offence). The essays on Eliot, Pound, Yeats and Edward Thomas are remarkable for their judiciousness, a judiciousness that depends on the root of the matter being for Sisson, as he said it was for Henry Vaughan, 'telling the truth'. It might be thought that a professed Anglican like Sisson would admire *Four Quartets*, but he did not (with the exception of *Burnt Norton*), regarding *The Waste Land*, 'Sweeney Agonistes' and 'Prufrock' as Eliot's finest poetic achievements. The merciless essay on Yeats has annoyed many admirers of the poet, among whom I number myself, though I was not among the annoyed; for Sisson, in drawing attention to the theatricality and posturing of rather too much of the verse, is saying what has to be said: 'The Stare's Nest by My Window' is a far truer poem than 'Sailing to Byzantium', and 'The Circus Animals' Desertion' a far greater one. Given his dislike of mere theatre and his interest in truth-telling, his estimate of Edward Thomas as 'one of the profoundest poets of the century' is unsurprising: 'All passion for the truth is revolutionary', he writes, and Thomas's work is no 'easy evocation of agreeable scenes' but 'a critique of what the world thinks of itself, and of its methods of thought'. The essay on Pound, in which he is rightly critical of Pound's foolishness in politics (though without touching directly on the poet's anti-semitism) and admiring of his rhythmical innovations, ends with a paragraph that in the light of recent events seems especially pertinent:

> If one had to name a single subject for the diverse material of the *Cantos*, it would be … usury. What is here exposed … is the monstrous aberration of a world in which reality is distorted … by the pull of a fictitious money. It is a noble subject and, when one reflects on it, may well be the only possible one for a long poem in our age. The interest of the subject is not likely to diminish …

Earlier in the essay, there are some remarks on the long poem which interest me because there is an omission that I think is telling: 'The satisfactory long poem is … a rarity in any age. *The Faerie Queene* is hardly one, although its readability and the lucidity of its language are much greater than is now commonly supposed; and anyway it is unfinished. Chaucer's *Troilus and Criseyde* is probably the most successful long poem in the language'. The omission, of course, is of *Paradise Lost*, and it always intrigued me that a man for whom the 'constitutional quarrels of the seventeenth century', and in whose understanding of English literature writers of the sixteenth and seventeenth centuries held so great a place, should never have addressed what remains by far the greatest long poem in English, despite the efforts of Pound, Eliot and Leavis to denigrate it, and Larkin, in his callow way, to pretend that it was 'boring'. Sisson did, however, in an entry in a book on writers' houses, speak well and in the main fairly of Milton (I teased him about it), and what he says is very instructive, but principally, I think, for what it says about Sisson. He is rather too deferential to the opinion of the 'superbly educated' Eliot and does not address the modernists' attack on Milton or question their misrepresentation of the coiling energy and variety of his verse: that reputedly monotonous 'organ-voice', that 'Chinese wall' of pentameter lines with a 'swat' on every even-numbered syllable. Milton is in fact the greatest master in English poetry of playing, by means of enjambement, syntax against metrical pattern to create a variety of differing movements, but the great modernists were so interested in the integrity of the individual line and in the principle of juxtaposition that they were unable or unwilling to appreciate what he was doing.

I wonder if this was not also the case with Sisson, who was strongly influenced by Pound in his versification. His preference, apparent in the essay I have mentioned, for *Samson Agonistes* over *Paradise Lost* is connected, I think, with the fact that its violently abrupted versification, especially in the choruses and some of Samson's soliloquies, is not unlike some of his own experiments. It is surely connected, too, with his clear preference for poetry that is spoken *in propria persona* (though there is no reason why this should necessarily have greater authenticity than poetry that is, or seems to be, more distanced from the poet's self), as well as with his taste for savagely uncompromising poetry that makes few or no concessions to what the world regards as beautiful, if indeed it does not go radically against it.

Such poems of his own as 'Eclogue', 'The Theology of Fitness', 'Human Relations', 'The Garden of Epicurus' or the fifth of the 'Autumn Poems' were revelatory for me since, like Milton's poetry, and in particular *Samson Agonistes*, they did not exist in that safe little aesthetic sphere that so much contemporary poetry seemed, and still seems, to exist in, and they were quite unlike anybody else's. There is a remark made by Richard Taruskin in connexion with J. S. Bach's harshest cantatas that is pertinent, where Sisson's poetry and its recognition, or lack of it, are concerned; for in setting such texts as 'My sins sicken me like pus in my bones; help me, Jesus, Lamb of God, for I am sinking in deepest slime', Bach used studiedly unbeautiful means, purposely making things difficult for the performers so that they could not, and cannot, create a beautiful and harmonious sound. Taruskin remarks (I rephrase his statement so that it refers to poetry and poetry lovers rather than to music and music lovers) that the idea that good and great poems can be ugly, or ugly poems good or great, is unthinkable to most poetry lovers – which shows, Taruskin goes on to say, 'how far we have strayed from the ancient aesthetic of the sublime'.

                And the hiss
My own malice makes of this wind
Gentle enough, in itself: I can imagine myself
As this tree but what consciousness
Should go with it – that,
Screeching neck, I am blind to.

('Autumn Poems, V')

What is pictured here is not unlike Alberto Giacometti's monstrous and terrifying small sculpture, 'Head on a Stalk'.

In the preface to his 'partial autobiography', Sisson writes that *On the Look-out* is 'the story of a man who, after some resistance, had to admit to being a poet.' It is a curious remark that I cannot help connecting with the 'growing deprivation' which, he writes in a fascinating couple of pages in *On the Look-out*, led him to be baptised and then confirmed in the Anglican communion, as well as with these lines from 'The Usk':

So I am come, stand in the cold tonight
The servant of the grain upon my tongue

In a deep way, Sisson's calling as a poet, his Christianity, his political beliefs were all one; they all sprang from the same primitive source, a source that lay below language, below ideas, below what is conscious: really in the body, which is why for him the incarnation was so important a myth. Or in the land – the soil – of England, with its 'spirits everywhere'. In all his writings, he seeks to elucidate his intuitions about this source, but in his poetry he more particularly seeks to embody them; which accounts in part for the extraordinary experimentation with broken syntax and with abrupt, dream-like transitions and juxtapositions that characterises so many of the 'new poems' from *In the Trojan Ditch* and so many of the poems in *Anchises* and *Exactions*; accounts also for the many images of ghosts, caves and the underworld, with Proserpine playing 'below the circle of (the) mind'. He discovered, in such poems as 'Somerton Moor', 'In insula Avalonia', 'The Herb-garden', 'Burrington Combe' and 'The Red Admiral', a powerful ambiguity that haunts the mind and once read is unforgettable.

Sisson wrote of Edward Thomas that he had not been given his rightful place, which may no longer be the case now. But Sisson's poetry – that 'unrecognised style' which 'was made by sorrow' – has certainly not been given anything near its due, and is unlikely to be given it in present circumstances. Like Milton's poetry, it goes quite beyond the restricted conceptions of poetry that are current now.

Sisson's oeuvre is enormous. In addition to the poetry, the autobiography and all the essays in criticism and political enquiry, there are the novels, and then the translations, of which my favourites are Virgil's *Aeneid* and Lucretius' *Poem on Nature* – not, I am afraid, *The Divine Comedy*, because it is my impression – perhaps mistaken, since my Italian is not at all good – that Dante does not write strongly end-stopped lines all the time, and plays syntax against metrical form to create a much more fluent movement than Sisson creates in English; as in his own poetry, Sisson seems to be interested chiefly in the energy of each line considered as a unit. But that is enough of my opinions. Here is the last stanza of 'The Red Admiral', in which strong enjambement, between subject and verb, is sensitively used:

> Its fingers lighter than spiders, the red admiral
> Considers, as I do, with little movement;
> With little of anything that is meant:
> But let the meaning go, movement is all.

Victoria Moul

C. H. Sisson's Art of Translation

The volume, scope and quality of C. H. Sisson's achievement as a translator is daunting: in addition to the substantial *Collected Translations* published in 1996, he produced complete versions of several major works including the *Aeneid* and the *Divine Comedy*. He published translations and original verse alongside one another in the 1974 collection *In the Trojan Ditch*, and the relationship between the practice of translation and his English poetry is a theme of several essays. In one, he describes translation as 'the best of literary exercises, perhaps the only serious one'.[1] Nor did his work as a translator pass unnoticed: John Pilling describes Sisson as 'one of the finest [translators] in contemporary literature'[2]; but his verse is also renowned for the 'Englishness' of its character, tone and range of allusion.[3] In this essay, I want to use Sisson's engagement with Latin poetry, and in particular with the tonal challenges of a major Latin poet – the Horace of the *Odes* and of the *Ars Poetica* – to explore the apparent paradox of this combination. In what ways did the study of this most archetypally Roman of poets contribute to the English identity of Sisson's verse?

In common with most poets whose work engages deeply and closely with the literature of another language, the distinction between translation, version and allusion in Sisson's poetry is a porous one. The short lyric, titled 'Hactenus arvorum cultus (*Georgics* II)', for instance, is printed in the *Collected Translations*. The title – the first three words of Virgil's second georgic – invites us to read this as a translation, but the poem really only begins from Virgil, and is far removed from him in tone:

---

[1] Sisson, *On the Look-Out* (Carcanet, 1989), p. 64. Alan Massey discusses this remark briefly (Alan Massey, '"Poet, Sergeant, Under Secretary": C. H. Sisson: *Collected Poems'*, *Agenda* 37 (1999), 69). Michael Schmidt also mentions the importance of translation to Sisson's poetry in his short article after Sisson's death in 2003 (Michael Schmidt, 'C. H. Sisson (1914-2003)' *PN Review* 30: 2 (2003), 3-4).

[2] John Pilling, 'The Strict Temperature of Classicism: C. H. Sisson', *Critical Quarterly* 21 (1979), 179.

[3] Richard Poole offers a particularly perceptive analysis of the English fabric of Sisson's work (Richard Poole, 'The Poetry of C. H. Sisson' *Agenda* 22 (1984), 32-56).

Up to now the fields
Have been ploughed and the stars
Sent us home to our cottages
At the end of the day.
There has been the vine,
Even on these hills, and the slow
Growing olive.
Not only the Cotswold shepherd
But I too, with even pace,
Treading where the wind can be heard
Or some horn perhaps. But this is over.
Nor even metal ringing
At the smithy, or a voice.
Water sucking the rotting
Piers,
The algae lifted
Tide by tide.
A single gull
Banking, back to the dead sea,
Cries.

'Up to now the fields / Have been ploughed and the stars' unmistakeably renders 'hactenus arvorum cultus et sidera caeli' (the first line of *Georgics II*). It even translates the Latin words in the same order as they appear in Virgil; but it does so to very different effect. What in the Latin are noun phrases (*'the cultivation of the fields and the stars of heaven'*) become verbal ones in the English poem, suggesting that such activities have now ceased: the fields have been ploughed, the stars have been our guides to daily life and work, but they no longer are.

The distance from the Virgilian text of what appears at first sight to be close translation is one aspect of the sadness of the English poem, its immanent loss. Part of what is declared 'over' (line 11) is the optimism, the joyous and determined fresh start of *Georgics* II. The vine and the slow-growing olive, the subjects of the *next* part of the poem in Virgil, the stuff of the future, are here, in a bleak version of England, already vanished. Even in this minor piece – it is almost a fragment – we see Sisson constructing his English tone, and indeed his English landscape, from the distance that he perceives between himself and a Latin classic. Sisson himself wrote of the difficulty of translating poetic tone in his essay on translating Dante:

Once one has taken a decision to translate into the language of one's own day [. . .] there is still the real problem, which, in all translations from another age, is that of *tone*. The problem presents itself to the translator – if he is any good – in an entirely concrete form. [. . .] In my experience, there is an identifiable moment when the translator can first say: I can translate a particular poet. Until that moment, all is uncertain. It is the point at which the first verses come to him convincingly in his own language; [. . .][4]

If the 'real problem' of translation is that of tone, then Horace must present a particular challenge, for the tonal range of his work is very wide: in the hexameter verse alone we find obscenity, invective and conversational verse – both satiric and philosophical. Amongst the extraordinarily rich and varied four books of lyric odes we find poems of friendship and of loss, and erotic and sympotic pieces, alongside those of high politics and epic pastiche.

This is not to mention the single most important piece of ancient poetry on the art of poetry itself. Sisson's translation of the *Ars Poetica*, published as *The Poetic Art* in 1975, is a major achievement, and at the heart of that achievement is the tone of the poem. Framed loosely as a long advisory epistle on poetic taste and craftsmanship, the poem is addressed to the young Piso brothers and their father, and Sisson's translation begins:

You may think nothing of zoological marvels
Or mind what a painter does to the human shape.
After Picasso, no one is shocked by distortions,
Yet, even so, there are rules to be observed.
Cork Street is not exempt from all derision
And there are books at least as bad as the pictures
– Flippant images out of a sick man's dream.
The serious work must do more than hang together.
It is no use saying: 'Painters and poet are equal'
– Of course – 'and equally free to use their invention.'
Of course. I invent things myself and am not against others.
That does not mean that I tolerate any stupidity
Of blots on canvas or words poured over a page.
(Sisson, 1-13)

This is far from being a close translation. Sisson's version of the opening

[4] C. H. Sisson, *In Two Minds: Guesses at Other Writers* (Manchester: Carcanet, 1990), 'Translating Dante', p. 195.

of Horace's poem sets aside almost entirely the guiding metaphor of the Latin, that of extravagant and unexpected pairings – inventions, according to Horace, which lack artistic decorum. Men and horses, women and fish, snakes and birds, tigers and lambs should not 'go together' – either sexually or as fantastic compound creatures. Artistic depictions of monsters and centaurs demonstrate a distasteful relish for the extraordinary figure over the complete and harmonious composition; unexpected matings are similarly a source of prurient interest. But what is most interesting about these examples is that they are not in fact grand guignol instances of the kind of thing about which Horace – or a young man trying to imitate Horace – would never dream of writing. On the contrary, we find examples of just this sort of motif in several of Horace's extant works, as well as those of his close and influential contemporaries.[5]

The opening to the *Ars Poetica* is treading a careful line: the poet employs a (by then) conventional poetic image of what is unconventional. The point is not that such images or pairings are *never* appropriate or decorous, but that they must be introduced thoughtfully, as part of a larger emotional or rhetorical structure, and not simply for effect, or titillation. The examples of the figure in the *Odes* and in Virgil are diverting – but also, importantly, their use makes sense. They are impossible combinations, and they are used to evoke impossibility, whereas Horace's opening lines here imagine such indulgences deployed without context or justification. Sisson has set aside what seems at first the most curious and distinctive element of these lines, precisely because in modern English the examples carry no such combined resonance of artful strangeness and rhetorical familiarity. Instead, he chooses to begin with an artistic motif (Picasso's distinctive distortions) that he appears to disparage – but the example is familiar, and derived moreover from one of the greatest artists of the previous generation. Sisson is not in these lines being merely reactionary: the point, just as in Horace, is that this now-familiar motif of strangeness and distortion is effective (and artistically successful) only when intelligently applied: 'The serious work must do more than hang together' (8).

This kind of feature is not confined to the opening lines. Sisson's *Ars Poetica* works out its 'modernism' in a consistently thoughtful manner. Where Horace cites Achilles as the prototypical hero (120), who must be recognisably 'Achillean' if he is to be introduced into a poem or a play, Sisson replaces him with Moses (123); Medea, Ino, Ixion, Io and Orestes (123-4)

---

[5] In Horace *Odes* I.33, for instance, the absurdities of sexual love and passion are compared to such impossible pairings.

become 'Adam and Eve' (127). The most striking aspect of Sisson's version is its direct and superficially straightforward tone:

> Either follow old tales or invent something probable.
> If you want to write about Moses, you had better not make him
> ridiculous;
> To say the least he held down a difficult job.
> And because you have forgotten the Ten Commandments
> It doesn't mean he was only after power.
> (122-126)

Once again, this is not a close translation; but like the opening of the poem, Sisson's version here responds creatively to the tonal poise of the Latin. There is a flattering complicity between author and reader in Horace's list of conventional adjectives to describe Achilles – 'impiger, iracundus, inexorabilis, acer' ('*swift, passionate in his anger, inexorable, fierce*', 121). The educated reader recognises the traditional attributes of the epic hero and sees that the line is close to pastiche (Horace, addressing the younger aspiring writer, describes what a poet must do and in so doing, does it in the space of a line). That the reader recognises what the author is up to is part of Horace's point: he is reminding the beginning poet that if he chooses to introduce a conventional character, he must retain enough of their traditional attributes to ensure that they are recognised. In a single line Horace both mocks and invokes epic grandiloquence and its rhetorical power. For all our readerly cleverness, it is hard *not* to be stirred by the monumental progression of adjectives in line 121, and by the sudden shift of Achilles (as seems proper) into the nominative, asserting himself – for all our enjoyment of the cliché – in his fitting role as the agent of the main verb in line 122.

Sisson's version of this passage is quite different: he alludes to Moses's reputation for persistence ('he held down a difficult job'), but there is no equivalent to the resounding series of adjectives in Horace, and his tone remains lower-key throughout. But as in the Latin, there is a doubleness to these lines. The reader is coaxed and flattered – we congratulate ourselves on knowing the story well enough to appreciate the humour of 'To say the least, he held down a difficult job' (124). But then we find ourselves caught out by an aside ('And because you have forgotten the Ten Commandments', 125). We think, of course, that we are thoroughly familiar with Moses, or Achilles, to the point of boredom – but *can* we remember each of the Ten Commandments? Do we know so much after all? Any well-read teenager – such as the Piso brothers Horace addresses in this poem – could produce the kind of knowing, slightly dismissive summary with which both Horace and Sisson begin: quick-tempered Achilles; Moses's difficult job. The poem – both poems – invite us to see that maturity demands that we think beyond that point, and read back behind the convention of these figures to the source of their cultural authority.

For Sisson, Moses is not just a clever and carefully worked-out replacement for Achilles; the poem is quite serious about its invitation to us – that is to speakers and readers of twentieth-century British English – to think carefully about our own inherited cast of heroes, of conventional protagonists. Sisson's translations from Horace – in this respect as in many others – purposefully create not just poems in English, but *English* poems, works which are thinking about Englishness in general and English literature in particular. This decision is played out not only in the systematic substitutions of the *Ars*, but most strikingly in the distinctive tone with which they are offered. There is a deprecation in 'Sisson's Horace' (of himself, of his calling, of his country, of his own authority) that is unmistakeably English:

Poets in our own tongue have left no subject untried,
And they haven't done their worst when they left the exotic behind
And found their plots nearer home, whether tragic themes
Or comedies based on familiar manners and ways.
The English could do as well in literature as in cricket
If their poets, one and all, did not have the fatal weakness
Of refusing to polish their work and waiting to see how it looks.
(282-288)

The English facility 'in cricket' translates Horace's 'virtute [. . .] clarisve [. . .] armis', '*in valour and glorious arms*' (289). Both Horace and Sisson are at once detached and affectionate in these lines; but it is a peculiarly English move to equate martial excellence with sporting achievement. For the attentive reader, the substitution both evokes and distances itself from England's own imperial history.

A particularly bold example of this Anglicising poetic deprecation is found in Sisson's version of Horace, *Odes* I.1. In Latin this is a finely judged but ultimately profoundly self-aggrandizing poem, especially given its position as the opening ode of the collection.[6] Sisson's translation transforms the poem's well-known conclusion. At the point at which the poet turns from speaking of others' preferred occupations and routes to glory (racing, politics, trade,

---

[6] Odes I, II and III were published together as a single collection. The unity of their conception is emphasised by the shared asclepiad metre of I.1 and III.30 – the only two odes in that form to be found in the first three books.

leisure, battle or hunting) to his own, Sisson writes:

> For me it is the ivy on my forehead,
> The trick of being a poet: the cold woods
> Alive with nymphs and satyrs, keep me out.
> I want no people if I have a flute,
> A lute, anything musical, a Muse
> To hand it to me. For I am a poet.

This is a much more muted version of poethood than we find in the Latin. In 'the ivy on my forehead' Sisson has elided entirely the phrase 'dis miscent superis', '*[the ivy garlands] mingle me with the gods above*'; and he makes no attempt to convey the significance of the ivy wreath as a mark of membership of the 'doctarum [. . .] frontium', literally the company of '*learned brows*', that is, of great poets. There is I think a self-consciousness, a hint of humour, in Horace's phrase 'dis miscent superis' – there are less elaborate ways to say 'set among' or 'ranked with' – but it is nevertheless audacious. Only the first rival pursuit, the Pindaric-style athlete, has been described with any comparable phrase ('palmaque nobilis / terrarum dominos evehit ad deos', 6) – a line that seems to *include* the possibility of exaltation, but does not quite say it: the palm lifts successful athletes towards the gods, but as lords of the earth, not heaven.

Still, Sisson's phrase 'the trick of being a poet' is self-deprecating in a quite different way from any hints of humour and reserve we may find in the Latin, and in the following lines he rewrites the meaning of Horace. The Latin says that the cool grove and the light choruses of the nymphs and satyrs – associated with Dionysus and so with poetic inspiration, and suggestive too of the countryside – 'me secernunt populo', '*keep me separate from the people*'. That is, literally, a version of the 'country retreat' motif: all the other forms of pursuit in the poem rely upon the busy-ness of civilisation, but the poet is content far away from the city. Sisson responds to the idea of separation and retreat, but his Horatian poet recasts the Latin. Here the poet is barred not only from the 'people' but even from the grove, the nymphs and the satyrs which are associated in Latin with the source of his inspiration:

> [. . .] the cold woods
> Alive with nymphs and satyrs, keep me out.
> I want no people if I have a flute,
> A lute, anything musical, a Muse
> To hand it to me. For I am a poet.

The final lines of the poem are much muted too. In the Latin, the series of grand Greek words – the names of the Muses, of Lesbos, and of 'barbiton', meaning a lyre – raises the register of the lines. Sisson's version of this passage works differently: although this is an unusually direct proclamation of poethood for a poet usually so marked by modesty, there is no hint of the grand public hymn here, as there is in Horace. But his light, playful lines, sliding from one similar sound to another – 'out', 'flute', 'a lute', 'anything musical', 'a Muse / To hand it to me' – respond recognisably to the aural self-consciousness of those big Greek words, and the poet's pleasure in them. That pleasure, we suspect, is right at the heart of Sisson's poethood, just as Greek words, Greek themes, Greek metres in Latin form lie at the heart of Horace's *Odes*, and so at the climax of this introductory poem.

The famous last two lines of Horace's poem – the major claim of laureate potential – have disappeared in Sisson's version. Both the hoped-for insertion amongst the '*lyric bards*' (that is, the existing canon of Greek lyricists) and the witty version of apotheosis ('*I shall strike the stars with my uplifted head*') are gone, and the whole sentence is reduced to a bare half line: 'For I am a poet'. Horace's depiction of poethood is at once a retreat (from various kinds of public life and approbation) and an assertive challenge. In his version of the poem, Sisson retreats finally even from Horace, and the English reserve of his ode has a characteristically double force: we recognise the distinctive clarity and self-deprecation of the 'Sissonian Horace'; but that characterisation is always conscious of its status as translation. Horace declares his alienation from various forms of popular achievement; Sisson's Horace is shut out, too, from the nymphs and Muses, the trappings of classical inspiration.

Occasionally, this mode of translation and its characteristic muting becomes something close to a confrontation with the Latin text. *Odes* III.30, linked to I.1 by its metre and theme, is perhaps Horace's boldest and least ironic statement of poetic power and immortality. Sisson's version of the most familiar central section of that poem is at first glance transparent in a way that is unusual among his translations of Horace:

non omnis moriar, multaque pars mei
vitabit Libitinam: usque ego postera
crescam laude recens, dum Capitolium
scandet cum tacita virgine pontifex.
dicar, qua violens obstrepit Aufidus
et qua pauper aquae Daunus agrestium
regnavit populorum, ex humili potens
princeps Aeolium carmen ad Italos
deduxisse modos.
(6-14)

62

I shall not die entirely, much of me
Will have no funeral, but anew will be
Praised and grow greater in the future time.
While Pontifex and silent Vestal climb
The Capitol, it shall be said that I
– Where Aufidus roars and yet the land is dry,
Where Daunus ruled the country people, great
Although he was not born to high estate –
First brought Greek lyricism to our verse.

(Odes III. 30. 7-15)

Despite the direct and unmodernised proper names, Sisson does several things here to work *against* the sense of the Latin. He rearranges the clauses so that the most important statement ('it shall be said that I', 11) is preceded by a subordinate clause ('While Pontifex and silent Vestal …', 10) and then interrupted by a very long, almost unfollowable, aside. This is quite different from the shape and movement of the Latin poem, which has a full stop after 'pontifex' (9) and a powerful new sentence to follow it: 'dicar, qua …'. He has also taken the clause 'ex humili potens' ('*a powerful man from a humble background*') with Daunus rather than with Horace himself (the natural reading in Latin), which further increases the length and complexity of that difficult sub-clause. The deceptively 'close' translation works to surprising effect: despite its brisk rhyme scheme, the English poem is complicated and slowed down by this series of decisions.

Similarly, Sisson chooses here, crucially, *not* to modernise the references to Roman culture as he so often does elsewhere. That decision goes some way towards distancing the translator – and the reader – from Horace's claim to endure: neither the priest nor the virgin climb the Capitol now. Sisson goes further: he makes no attempt to explain the 'tacita virgine' of the Latin (the Vestal Virgin), calling her simply 'silent Vestal'; and he writes 'Pontifex', capitalised, without glossing the term as a priest. Similarly, he offers no contemporary or more intelligible equivalent for Daunus and Aufidus: Daunus was a legendary king of Apulia, where Horace was born, and Aufidus the region's major river, so both clauses refer specifically to the glorification, along with Horace, of the (otherwise rather obscure) land of his birth.

As is often the case, the translation is most distinct – most Sissonian, least Latin – in its closing lines:

Melpomene, the honour this deserves
Is yours, and yet the laurel crown which serves
To mark the triumph, properly belongs
To the executive who wrote the songs.

Only in the very final line does Sisson seal his divergence in tone and effect from the Latin with a significant departure in the literal details of his translation: there is no hint in Horace of the self-deprecatory tone that marks the English phrase 'the executive who wrote the songs'.

Sisson's decision to retain the grand and exotic Latin terms of the poem is interesting because it makes us much more conscious than we usually are when reading 'Sisson's Horace' that the text is a translation. The moving (and humorous) force of that final line – albeit moving and humorous in quite a different way from Horace's Latin – is in the implied acknowledgment of the limits of translation. Horace would never have called himself an 'executive' – Sisson does so here not only because he is writing, as always, as himself, an English poet who does not like to boast; but also because he writes as a translator. The surprising ending is, after all, of a piece with the unusually 'close' translation of the rest of the poem: *both* the exotic terms for long-lapsed practices of uncertain significance *and* the self-conscious and unHoratian understatement of the final line remind us of the limitations of translation as well as of its power.

Whereas in *Odes* III. 30 (and, to a lesser extent, in I. 1) Sisson's translations and their distinctive tone – the 'Sissonian Horace' – seem to limit the authority of his poetic voice and downplay the claim to immortality, his version of *Odes* II. 14 (the 'Postumus' ode) works instead to moderate the total eclipse of the addressee. It is Sisson's lovely rendering of this ode – perhaps the finest of his translations of Horatian lyric, and printed, fittingly, as the final poem of *In the Trojan Ditch* – with which I want to end.

The years go by, the years go by you, nameless,
I cannot help it nor does virtue help.
　Wrinkles are there, old age is at your elbow,
　Death on the way, it is indomitable.

Not if you choose, as you will choose, to doctor
Yourself with hope, will you weep out your pain.
　The underworld is waiting. There are monsters
　Such as distended you before you died.

The subterranean flood is there for every-
one who has taken food and drink on earth.
　A light skiff will put out, you will be on it –
　And, win the pools, you still will go aboard.

The blood dried on you and you came home safely
– Useless. You blew out an Atlantic storm.
– No need to fear the wind, it can do no harm.
It brings you where you will be brought at last.

The dark, the black and, in the blackness, water,
A winding stream, it will not matter to you.
    The fifty murderesses are there, the toiler,
    Exhaustion beyond hope, condemned to dreams.

Your house, your wife, and the familiar earth,
All will recede, and of the trees you prune
    Only the cypress follow you, ill-omened.
    You were here briefly, you are here no more.

The heir you leave is better than yourself,
What you kept closest he will throw away.
    Your books are on the pavement, and his laughter
    Sounding like broken glass through all the rooms.

Horace's ode is in many respects a rather personal poem, with an edge
of *ad hominem* reproach: Postumus's wealth and greed, it is implied, are
particularly foolish given the certainty of death. Sisson's translation is close
but expansive – the final lines of each of the last four stanzas are wholly
or largely additions to the Latin. But Sisson's 'you', the addressee of the
poem, is – at once both wittily and sadly – here 'nameless'. The name
'Postumus', suggestive in English of our reputation after death and repeated
to solemn effect in the first Latin line ('eheu fugaces, Postume, Postume'),
has been erased. The shape of the opening line in English leaves it ambiguous
whether it is 'you' (that is, the addressee) or the 'years' who are nameless,
an uncertainty that reproduces to some degree the complex word order and
delayed agreements of Horace's lyric stanza.

eheu fugaces, Postume, Postume,
labuntur anni nec pietas moram
    rugis et instanti senectae
        adferet indomitaeque morti:

(1-4)

Word order is also key to the ambiguities of the Latin. The meaning of this
opening sentence is that piety ('pietas', 2) does *not* offer or bring ('adferet',
4) any delay ('moram', 2) to the inevitability of death. But both the subject

65

('pietas') and the object ('moram') of the sentence, as well as its governing 'nec' ('not'), are tucked away together in line 2. When we finally reach the main verb in line 4 it *does* 'bring' us directly to death that cannot be overcome ('indomitaeque morti', 4). It is not that the sentence *means* one thing but suggests another; rather it says one thing while using its complex word order to mime that same message in a different way. What we grasp, most strongly, is both the grudgingness of the admission, and its overwhelming force. Sisson's syntax does not work in quite this entangled way: the clause about virtue and the clause about the inevitability of death are placed in separate sentences. But the troubling near-rhyme of 'at your elbow' and 'indomitable', and the lingering, oddly-stressed drawn-out sound of those phrases captures something of both the internal resistance and the inevitability of the Latin sentence.

We have already seen that Sisson's handling of that opening stanza suppresses some of the *ad hominem* force of the Latin address: he includes a poetic I ('I cannot help it', 2) where the Latin does not; but the 'you' of his version is more general. The poet speaks to – and for – all of us, and this is central to his translation as a whole. As so often, it is in the final stanza of the poem that we find the greatest changes and the most distinctively Sissonian tone. Here, Sisson has removed the evocative (but typically Roman) imagery of wine; instead we have books – perhaps more likely as prized possessions of the poet than of Postumus – and the vaguer 'what you kept closest'. His most significant transformation is of the final two lines. A very literal translation might read: '*[the heir] will stain the pavement with a fine wine, too good for priests' dinners.*' 'Cena' is a very ordinary Roman word, more suited to prose than poetry, and this stanza is the most distinctively *Roman* of the whole poem, as Nisbet and Hubbard point out.[6]

One of the most remarkable features of Horace's odes is the power of their final word. In this poem, as so often, Horace somehow manages to load a bare, unevocative and unpoetic noun – here 'cenis', '*dinners*' – with emotive force. Unsurprisingly, Sisson cannot match this brevity and concentration. His replacement is nevertheless effective, suggesting both the waste and destruction of the physical building ('broken glass'), the scale of what will be lost ('all the rooms'), and the heir's triumph over the addressee ('his laughter'). But Horace's poem, with its tighter emotional restraint, focuses our attention upon the obscurity of the addressee after his death precisely by his total eclipse: it is the heir, not Postumus, who is the agent of the entire

---

[6] 'The poem has moved from the scenes of Greek poetry to the prosaic world of Roman society' (R. G. M. Nisbet and Margaret Hubbard, *A Commentary on Horace Odes, Book II* (Clarendon Press, 1978), p. 240.)

final stanza in Latin. Sisson's version cannot quite bear to discard Postumus so bluntly: 'the heir you leave is better than *yourself*', 'what *you* kept closest', '*your* books are' – the verse rings with the personal pronoun. This reluctance is closely linked to the patterns we observed in the first stanza, and the books on the pavement in this one: Sisson's unRoman Horace speaks here less of the rich and frivolous Postumus than he does of himself.

I have been writing of Sisson's delicacy of tone, and especially the 'Englishness' of that tone, in translating Horace, the most *Roman* of poets. In his essay on Sisson's poetry, Richard Poole ends by discussing the final lyric from the sequence titled 'Burrington Combe', a particularly fine poem that he considers both 'quintessentially English' (55) and, for all its 'commanding simplicity', 'tonally elusive' (56). It is interesting, then, that this lovely poem seems to be itself a response to *Odes* II.14:

When I walk out there will be nothing missing
That I can see;
The pond will be there with its fish,
The rosemary

Spreading itself over the garden
As if still aided by my hand;
The mulberry-tree I planted, and the cherry,
The old apple-tree and

The plums stretching up against the wall
Over which the church-tower still looks;
Starlings and swallows, the swans flying over,
And always the rooks.

And that distance into which I shall have vanished
Will still be there;
It was always dear to me, is now
In the thickening air.

No distance was ever like this one
The flat land with its willows, and the great sky
With the river reflecting its uncertainty
But no more I.

Poole is surely right to consider this poem 'quintessentially English' both in its attitude towards the landscape, and in its poetic register (we are reminded perhaps particularly of Hardy's 'Afterwards'). But those stable trees, outlasting the poet, derive from Horace; and the final line ('But no more I') is related to one of Sisson's expansions of the Latin ode ('You were here briefly, you are here no more', 24). Death is inevitable, and not even beloved trees will follow you; but Sisson has transformed the intransigence of Horace's thought – 'I shall have vanished', 'But no more I', the dead take nothing with them – into a distinctively English mirror-image of that idea: the landscape that is left behind *will* endure ('And that distance . . . / Will still be there'). Much of the poem is a kind of imaginative meditation on Horace's single phrase 'harum quas colis arborum' (22), and ultimately a refutation of it: 'those trees you tended' will in this most English of poems continue to grow 'as if still aided by my hand' (6). We could say the same of Horace – always still there; and as I hope to have demonstrated, Sisson was of these great poems the most careful and intelligent cultivator and guardian.

Patrick McGuinness

Sisson and Maurras

Late style came early to C. H. Sisson. We might say it was his first and only style, and he stayed true to it across the range of his concerns: from poetry and translation to critical, political and historical prose.

Reading Sisson's essays for *New English Weekly*, essays that he wrote between 1937 and 1949, from his early twenties to his mid-thirties, we are struck by the precocious maturity of his cultural politics. By *maturity* I don't mean that his cultural politics are middle of the road or even consensual – they are not – but rather that they reach, early on, a point beyond which they do not advance (and do not wish to), merely expand their range and enlarge their sphere of application. They also deny themselves the status of ideals; first because they are not experienced *as* ideals, and second because they do not see politics of any kind as the proper place for ideals. Sisson's cultural politics are, in the specific sense of that devalued word, *reactionary*, and we can situate him in a tradition of European-influenced but specifically *English* reactionary writers and thinkers, chief among whom is T. E. Hulme, surely a defining presence in Sisson's early thought.

Like Hulme's, Sisson's reaction was forged in opposition to what he perceived as Leftist orthodoxy, seen as dangerous not just for its actual politics, but for its totalising assumptions about culture, democracy, governance and human nature. Hulme's battle was with Bloomsbury metropolitanism, its pacifism and the way much of that pacifism was underwritten (financially, but also culturally) by notions of class superiority. Hulme's polemics against the likes of Bertrand Russell came with bracing titles like 'Why we are in favour of this war: the case against "another cucumber sandwich"'. Hulme's politics may have been reactionary, but he never fell for the anti-democratic, militaristic, anti-Semitic or nation-and-race-based varieties some of his contemporaries played with. Even in the trenches he displayed none of the anti-German xenophobia that characterized one strand of the English intellectual class. And democracy, that bugbear of reactionary modernism, was still the only viable system for Hulme: 'No theory that is not fully moved by the conception of justice asserting the equality of men, and which cannot offer something to all men, deserves or is likely to have a future'. For Hulme, the 'Religious Attitude' was not about the existence of God (a 'secondary notion' apparently, discussion of which was mainly 'chatter') but about setting abstract standards – religion, authority, monarchy – by which a generally messy world could be ordered. It seems to me that Sisson too had this idea: what Hulme would have called the 'cinders' or 'the mud', on which one could only gain purchase through the rational application of regulatory systems, from railway lines (one of Hulme's favourite analogies) to religions. Sisson would have added the civil service to Hulme's list.

One proposed these systems not because one believed in their ineffable power or even rightness, but because one believed in the need to believe in them. This element of reactionary modernism we can partly attribute, in early twentiety-century thought, to Charles Maurras, the French thinker who profoundly influenced a generation of British modernists, from Eliot and Hulme to David Jones and Saunders Lewis in Wales. The young Sisson seems to have been of a Hulmean cast of mind, not just in his idea of the connectedness between culture and politics, or in his blend of Europeanism and Englishness, but in his quite nuanced ability to pick and choose what, in the Maurrassian scheme, might work in England. When Sisson writes 'England' he usually means England. Reading *The Avoidance of Literature* we are struck by Maurras's recurrent presence. Maurras in fact turns up wherever the politics/culture nexus is evoked, and always as an inspiring but flawed example. Part of Sisson's precocious maturity (if that isn't a contradiction) is that even in the first essays on Maurras he is quite remarkably aware of the danger of cross-applying Maurrassian thought and solutions to British contexts. One of the most noticeable aspects of Sisson's treatment of Maurras, apart from his being unafraid to reject elements of the Maurrassian world-view, is the absence of any reference to Maurras's virulent anti-Semitism, and generally to Maurras's connections to the French nationalist far-right in its less intellectual manifestations. Maurras is instead treated from the beginning as a writer and thinker engaged in a total culture and a total politics, but also as someone above the fray. The engagement with Maurras is not necessarily adulatory – indeed Sisson early on qualifies and corrects and dismisses elements of Maurras's thought – but it is always conducted without reference to the nastier side of Maurras's activities: his incitement to murder (for which Maurras was imprisoned), the streetfighting, his lionization, happily accepted, by the early fascists (whom Maurras never joined, but certainly encouraged), his rhetoric of cultural and national purification, knowingly targeted at a less erudite and less 'classical' audience than the European conservative intelligentsia.

Sisson is not the only one – T. S. Eliot and even Hulme had overlooked the race-hate propounded by *Action française*, in part because Maurras himself professed not to believe in racial theory or in any ideas of racial superiority. Maurras described his own anti-Semitism as 'anti-sémitisme d'état', or 'state anti-semitism', something abstract and political, a matter of ideas about governance, state institutions and national identity – in other words an 'intellectual' position, something 'rational'. Maurras claimed to find Nazi anti-Semitism barbaric, not because he objected to anti-Semitism *per se*, but because he found its basis in racial theory primitive and atavistic. It is part of the self-exonerating fiction of French anti-Semitism that, being cultural rather than racial, it was of a fundamentally different order from that of the Germans, even when, as often, it expressed itself in the same racial ways. Looking back on the engagement of British intellectuals with Maurras, it is perhaps unsurprising that the high-point of his influence should have come in the inter-war period – T. S. Eliot in *The Criterion*, Middleton Murry in *The Adelphi*, Sisson in *New English Weekly*. Maurras appealed to those modernist writers who refused to think of literature and literary values as chasmically divided from the culture, from the state and its institutions, and generally from the spiritual life of the nation. It was in part because it counteracted the totalizing cultural politics of socialism that the totalizing cultural politics of Maurras appealed to a certain kind of British writer.

A *cultural politics* is what we see in Sisson's attachment to the church, the monarchy, and the civil service, all of them forms of order imposed on a chaos, but also *regulating* democracy and not, as Maurras would have wanted, *replacing* it. This is the Hulmean in Sisson, a specifically English suspicion of the grand scheme, the total plan, a willingness to work with what is fallen and imperfect. These imperfect and imperfectly regulating systems are also greater than the sum of their imperfections – the banality of the monarch in person is made up for by the binding nature of its pageantry, the dullness of the civil service is its strength, because if it were not dull it might not be either *civil* or a *service*, the Church of England, a pragmatic melding of religion and state, and the only church designed for agnostics, is an expression of spirituality rather than its home.

Of course, I am putting words into Sisson's mouth here, but I exaggerate because I mean to express that what I enjoy most about him is the scrupulously downbeat and disabused way in which he defends his institutions. Those barely enthusiastic, pre-emptively jaded essays about poetry and culture and politics resemble many of his poems and translations (I think especially of his spartan version of Dante), where there is a deliberate roughness, a refusal to rise rhetorically, and retreat from formal perfection. A conservative, perhaps a reactionary, almost certainly a believer in the class system, though not, it must be noted, in its rigidity or even fairness, one can think of no poet or critic less suited either to the materialist right of the post-Thatcher Britain, nor of the slippery pseudo-left of Blairism and since. It is hard to imagine a less appropriate poet laureate than C. H. Sisson, despite the probability that he alone among his contemporaries really *believed* (spiritually, institutionally, culturally) in the post.

71

Sisson represents what Hulme would have called 'a certain kind of Tory', something that means pretty much nothing these days, but which played its role in the development of a conservative cultural politics that tends to be forgotten in the crude binarism of the left/right narrative, as well as the corporatist post-ideological culture we have today. What is interesting and valuable about this brand of conservative cultural politics is that it is essentially modernist, not just in its poetics but in its ideological and cultural bearings. It does not tarry, the way Eliot and Pound did, with the radical right. Sisson is, for the record, very sharply aware of the brutality and viciousness of Nazism, and is attuned to its threat very early on. It is not the conservatism of, say, Larkin or Betjeman, and it is barely part of the 'native tradition' of British poetry (whatever we mean by that). It represents a sort of lost or marooned tradition in British cultural politics, and Sisson's essays exemplify it in its purest, as well as its most isolated, form. Sisson's political essays are among the most deep-reaching engagements any British poet has shown with the world of politics in the twentieth century – not just political theory or political ideology, but politics in all its mess and slop and chaos. It is also, despite a few fluctuations and changes of emphasis, extraordinarily consistent, and that consistency can be traced through Sisson's relationship with Maurras.

From his earliest essay on Maurras, in 1937, through the 1950s (Maurras stood trial in 1944 for 'complicity with the enemy', and was imprisoned until 1952, dying soon after his release), right up to his last essay on Maurras in 1976, Sisson has a lifetime's engagement with Maurras, and it seems that in the 70s he began to write a book on him. It is especially brave, given Maurras's appalling reputation after the war, that Sisson should be so oddly loyal to this figure who, for all his extremism and for the ugliness of much of what he espoused, was made a scapegoat for all sorts of darker and more inconvenient truths about French involvement with fascism. Perhaps the most surprising of Sisson's essays on Maurras was published in *PN Review* as 'Looking Back on Maurras'. Here Sisson describes the French writer's continuing 'seduction', and wonders why Maurras still hasn't 'fallen into place, with Eliot, say, or Yeats, as a figure to whom I acknowledge a debt from a distance'. It is a pretty brazen defence of Maurras – defence by omission, certainly (nothing on Maurras's anti-semitism, his rabble-rousing, his profoundly anti-democratic nationalism) – but also defence by selective contextualization: the Dreyfus affair is described, for instance, as a question of whether 'the considerations of justice to an individual should take precedence over the welfare and safety of [a] state' threatened by 'a recurrently hostile foreign power'. This quite extraordinary description of the Dreyfus case is so slanted that one barely needs Sisson to clarify his own bias when, in the next sentence, he describes the 'liberal answer' to this so-called dilemma as E. M. Forster's 'if I had to choose between betraying my country and betraying my friends, I hope I should have the guts to betray my country'. It is a crude caricature of both the Dreyfus case and of what was at stake, and as Sisson presents it – in 1976! – it is also an absolutely unreconstructed reactionary alibi for one of French history's ugliest chapters.

Sisson may or may not believe his own caricature, but the point of his essay is to turn Maurras into a more idealistic, more principled and, one might say, more quixotic figure than he was. Sisson allows Maurras his flaws – notably his tendency to romanticize his native Provence and to disregard the realities of industrial and city life in pursuit of a classical dream – but they are flaws that appear designed to distract attention from the altogether more serious and unpalatable stratum of Maurras's ideology. For instance, Sisson quotes a letter from Maurras to Barrès fulminating against Jews and Protestants ruining Nîmes as an example of 'how narrow Maurras's basic sympathies were, how narrow, really, the world of his imagination'. The more logical deduction would be to see that letter as evidence of Maurras's anti-Semitism and sectarianism, not to mention his belief in a racially, culturally and religiously pure France. But Sisson leaves that out, preferring instead to guide the reader towards a relatively innocent interpretation of the letter.

It puzzles me how Sisson, who would not tolerate such absolutism himself, and who indeed conceives of the whole relationship between culture and the state, the institutions and their bureaucracies, as existing to ensure that such absolutism and intolerance are kept away from power, is so ready to overlook it (and so much else) in Maurras. There is something in Maurras that Sisson finds himself uncharacteristically able to romanticize – his 'complex and elaborately-related dogmatisms', and his life of 'self-abnegation' certainly, but also the totality and interconnectedness of his cultural politics; in short, their impossibility and probably also their undesirability too.

Sisson also romanticizes Maurras's Provence. His poem 'Martigues', the opening poem of *In the Trojan Ditch*, is about a visit to Maurras's birthplace in 1973. This trip was connected to the plan to write a book on Maurras. The poem does not mention him but is full of his presence: surely Maurras is the 'old friend/ Whom I have never seen/ Your ghost is my beginning'. The poem also evokes the limpid lines, the nostalgia and the classicism of Maurras's own poetry, as well as its décor, its flora (rose laurel, myrtle, laurel, roses, olives, thyme) and its informing presences: 'Pallas Athene', but also the fishermen speaking their Latinate *patois*. Maurras was, it is often forgotten, a significant and underrated poet, albeit a constricted and repetitive one, and a formalist in the tradition of the *école romane* founded by Mallarmé's rival, Jean Moréas, as an alternative to the 'foreign' formlessness of Symbolism.

73

Sisson's free verse 'Martigues' is a sort of recalcitrant reckoning with Maurras. It evokes the Maurassian world of light, continuity and order, but disturbs it too, by admitting its attractions and its beauties while never being convinced of their existence except in the mind. There is a moment in the poem when the speaker describes growing roses, myrtle and thyme in his English garden, as if the transposed flora of Martigues, like Maurras's ideas, cannot grow, or cannot grow in the same way, in the 'garden where I made my home'. 'In Somerset I crumble up the soil/ And linger on a terrace looking south'. That symbolism of the soil, Maurras's great (pseudo-) elemental bedrock of national consciousness, is used by Sisson not to embed certainties but to uproot them. It is a fine poem for the way it plays with the chthonic territorialism of Maurras, allows itself to be drawn to it, only to let it crumble into a peculiarly Sissonian fade-out of disillusionment and tired pragmatism. That opt-out from idealism is the poetic correlative of Sisson's essays on Maurras, and perhaps indeed of all his essays on politics and culture.

Another, earlier, poem, 'Maurras Young and Old', imagines Maurras as Maurras would doubtless have imagined himself:

> The Latin light
> Showed on the Mediterranean hills
> A frugal culture of wine and oil.
> Unobserved in their fog the British
> *toto divisos orbe*
> Propounded a mystery of steam
> In France they corrected the menus
> Writing for biftec: beef steak.
> Monsieur Maurras noted the linguistic symptoms
> He noted, beyond the Drachenfels
> The armies gathering.

The mix of hero-worship, lack of critical perspective, limp and clichéd list of linguistic slippage that reads like a menu of modernist gripes against modernity, idealized archaism and glib insertion of sweeping historical symptoms of decline (so Poundian) – all these make the poem thoroughly unconvincing and second-rate. What distinguishes Sisson's best poetry is of a piece with what makes his prose so significant: a strange roughness, almost a willed clumsiness, a fear of perfection, of rhetorical raids, a retreat from polish, a deliberately-advertised suspicion of formalism and neatness of phrasing.

What 'Maurras Young and Old' reminds us of, by being so inferior to, is Geoffrey Hill's *Mystery of the Charity of Charles Péguy*. Altogether differently imagined, and on the opposite side in the Dreyfus affair, Péguy is not unrelated to Maurras in his mix of politics and mysticism, and most especially perhaps in the exemplary nature of his failure. Hill wrote his great Péguy poem in part because he was not afraid to mix the politics and the mysticism into poetry. Sisson would have been unable to do that, however close he came to romanticizing and even idealizing Maurras. After writing that 'Maurras founded his politics on his esthetics, and that is a lunacy', he must have known there was no great poem to be written about Maurras. I'm inclined to think that Sisson wrote his Maurras poem in his essays, and that he wrote it over and over.

Editor's note:

Agenda Editions / André Deutsch published Geoffrey Hill's The Mystery of The Charity of Charles Péguy *in 1983.*

Charlie Louth

C. H. Sisson

For someone who doubted the existence of personality, he was pretty distinct. That is not surprising, in itself. He would have said the distinctness was nothing to do with him. He did say it, and added that his words weren't either:

> the amiable man
> Lying in bed with the morning paper,
> Or surly old devil who bites your head off:
> Shadows and shells, you could say no more,
> They are no more me than my words.
>
> ('Where?')

But most poets are like their poems, are their words, in important ways, though they cannot be quite like them. And there are ways in which his poems are like him and he was like his poems.

*

He was a very physical man, though perhaps not as the phrase might usually be understood. He needed the proof of his own senses. And his senses were like an extension of his mind. Once when he had a new car we were fiddling with some of the things it could do. It would light your cigarette, if you had one. Egged on, he pushed the lighter in to heat up, but when he pulled it out again there was no sign that anything had happened. Not having a cigarette, he touched his finger into it and the car filled with the stench of burnt skin. It was a nasty burn. Wondering whether it was hot, his curiosity reached into his fingertips. Probably he poked his finger in a bit further than he meant to.

*

'Neatness', he says of Robert Graves, 'is one of the elements of literature'. His poems could be neat, but much more often they are awkward, won't settle into a pattern, don't quite fit their forms. They suggest something but don't carry on with it. They convince by being themselves, by keeping a kind of roughness, or hesitance, by doing what they have to do. In 'Natural History'

76

he quotes Montesquieu: 'Un homme qui écrit bien n'écrit pas comme on a écrit, mais comme il écrit, et c'est souvent en parlant mal qu'il parle bien.'

*

A driving memory: there was something twitching by the side of the road, a hare. It had been hit but not killed. He stopped the car and got out, went to look, fetched a spanner from the boot to put it out of its suffering. He did what was necessary but he did not do it cleanly, there was a clumsiness to his gestures, the thing could not be well done perhaps. But he did what had to be done. He wasn't good with his hands, they were fumbling and sure at once.

*

In his writings he is fond of quoting from nursery rhyme or popular song: 'Hink, spink, the puddings stink'. He called nursery rhymes 'the original and most important element in poetic education'. There are parts of his poems which lapse into inarticulacy – 'Hey down' – or chanting, into words which work not so much through their sense as through their gestures, through being 'half dumb' as he calls himself in 'Ellick Farm'. Movement enters the poems as what is more meaningful, more truthful, than anything that can quite be named in words and connected in syntax. Picking at Donald Davie's notion of 'articulate energy' he says that 'any form which finds its way into human speech, however articulated or disjointed, may find a place in poetry'.

*

Once, when for some reason the word 'attitude' came up, he said that really of course attitude is: and threw his arms and legs out grotesquely as he came round to his place at the table.

*

'In the end they seem to be less awkwardnesses than aspects of his speaking mind, like a particular lurch or other movement which is habitual to some bodies. The rhythm of the verse, with its hesitations, sudden speeds, and pauses which are almost silences, is the very rhythm of thought.' What he says here about Hardy's 'awkwardnesses of expression' has something also to do with him. His own awkwardnesses are not of diction or rhyme but more of shape and line, the 'irregularities and straggling rhythms' he admired in Edward Thomas. As he speaks his mind, says what he has to, 'something not

77

altogether easy to say', it takes on a particular fall, asserts an independence which yet recognizes the way things are. 'What you might call your words, in a borrowed rhythm, would not be your words.' As it is, the poems are precarious, often only just hanging together, and reading them one is forced to give oneself over to their movements. The movements are not elegant, but they can be delicate. In 'The Red Admiral' the whole poems shifts and trembles like the butterfly, its changes are also those of memory and the considering mind:

> A woman, a horse, and a walnut-tree: old voices
> Out of recessed time, in the cracks,
> It may be, where the plaster has crumbled.
> But the butterfly hugs the blue lias.

Yes, 'we are in the depths of the poet's mind' and what we find there is not so much 'images', as he says is the case with the 'lynxes and leopards' of Pound's *Cantos*, as a kind of flickering: 'movement is all'. Authenticity is not a word I can imagine him liking much, and the only time he uses it that I can think of he ascribes it to an unnamed 'French writer'. But authenticity is what breathes out of the poems, if not as an aim then as a consequence. The best ones are instinct with their own identity. 'Much more than the ear – the touch, the sight, the pulse itself – enters into our perception of rhythm', and all this enters our perception of the poems.

*

Impossible to talk about him without talking about her. Who passed him her watch to wind – 'It won't work for me'. Who was a great teller of stories, never the same one twice, whereas his we heard over and over again. Whose hands, if not good at winding her watch, were full of knowledge, were elegant and practical at once, rubbing open pea-pods, smoothing out a piece of mending with the thumb. Her memory was much better than his. Perhaps his experiences became so much part of him that he was simply altered and had no need of the exact memory. Once he was talking of his uncles and aunts. One uncle apparently died falling off a stool in a bar. She remembered this, as told by his father. He said he thought it quite likely: this uncle was interested in poetry and had some very good books. Falling off a bar stool was about right, and served him right for getting involved in poetry. Then another uncle, a bank inspector, who put his head in the oven, after he retired, over a woman.

Difficult to talk about him without talking about the house, its garden sloping towards and then stopping abruptly over the Levels where the Parrett winds its slow way between raised banks or, in winter, bursts them and makes a bright sheet of water holding the sky. Uneven steps go down under the apple-trees; in one corner the 'little man', a grinning Priapic statue, stands guard near other apple-trees and near a level place where in summer sometimes he would have his afternoon sleep on an old army camp-bed he had brought back from the war. The church-tower reaches over the wall, loud with bells or starlings. The garden is badly overgrown now, half-abandoned, the pond choked and fishless, the beds more and more encroached on, plumes of fennel in unlikely places, everything spreading and merging, the rosemary quite out of control. It was never trim exactly, had a *désinvolte* look, was accompanied rather than curbed, 'aided', but now it has gained the upper hand. Inside things are still much as they were, so that it's easy to imagine him sitting at the bottom of the stairs to put on his shoes, or sprawled on the hearth-rug and laying a fire, or in his chair with the newspaper open on his knees. The house is still full of them as well as empty and surrounds us more with presence than with absence. They loved their house, the place, kept time at bay there with cups of tea at precise intervals, and some of the order persists, the repose. The house, open to the elements driving at it across the flats, subject to the shifting light, rests firmly on the hillside. 'There is no meaning except in terms of a time and a place.'

*

What I am trying to say is that the gestures of the verse are like the gestures of the man. 'The poet literally feels his way forward, and when the moment comes when he is no longer touching something he has either finished his poem or is left with a broken piece in his hands.' Perhaps there is some connexion between the way one is moved and the way one moves. The poems are all things he was moved to write and one can catch his voice in them and perhaps cadences of his body too. If poetry is a disburdening, as for him at least it was, then this implies a movement which though not elegant, not unconstrained, brings with it a certain freedom, an easing. And this is how awkwardness can also be a sort of grace.

*

A lot of him though is hard to find in the writings. In his last years he wanted to die and in that he was true to the poems, but there was a great enjoyment, relish even, of the things of life. The disappointment that runs through the poems came from a deep knowledge of what contentment was. And there were jokes and hilarity. I remember his face lit by laughter when a paper, fetched just in time in the interval between his getting on the train and its leaving, and handed up to him, somehow fell down the gap between carriage and platform.

Fleur Adcock

Alfred

i.m. Alfred Robinson, 1861-1934

Suddenly I've outlived my grandfather:
the one for whom I was unique, his only
grandchild, although eleven more were to come.

An infant bundle on his bedside rug,
I must have heard the not yet fathomable
murmurs of his farewell to my mother.

'Tell her about me when she's older', he said.
She did better than that: she gave me
his complete Shakespeare, 1928,

bought the following year, on Shakespeare's birthday –
just the kind of thing I might have done.
The print is tiny, to my ageing eyes.

Did he find it easier to read
in the clear light he'd emigrated to
from murky Manchester than I do here, now?

Thirty-seven plays, in eight-point type.
I read them in my teens, lying on the carpet
in my bedroom, and ticking them off as I went:

Hamlet (tick), Macbeth (tick), Henry the Fifth (tick) –
goodbye, Grandpa – The Tempest (tick) – thank you –
and the sonnets (tick)! Goodbye (tick), goodbye...

Stephen Romer

Heimkunft

Ruhig glänzen indeß die silbernen Höhen darüber,
  Voll mit Rosen ist schon droben der leuchtende Schnee.
– Hölderlin

And then one day the young master returns
from a dark place
and birdsong leads the wanderer in
and the cat yawns and curls again
in the headiness of this instant
the house is fragrant
with woodsmoke and honeysuckle

which is a kind of accomplishment.

Returning from dogma
home to the humane
he lays aside
knapsack, alpenstock and hat,
goes straight to the piano
sits bolt upright and picks out
1 2 3 of the *Wohltemperirte*.

The *Bildungsroman*, his own,
is unopened on the table,
but let it be, let
the elevation last – for it must fall –
a moment longer.

The blue dome is tense, the gods are close.

Everything is possible.

[First published in: *Revue LISA/LISA e-journal*, Vol. VII – No. 3 | 2009, Online since 19 May 2009, URL: http://lisa.revues.org/index70.html]

Evohe! Evohe!

In a peal of vowels
before bedtime
the figure dancing in the downpour
sets up her *ololuge*
just beyond the porch,
a Maenad in the lightnings
Evohe! Evohe! Io! Io!
Look at me! Look at me!
Twined in her hair
a stick of celery
'as used in the Games at Corinth'
– but what is that to her? –
she is danced by the storm…

And I say to the seven-year-old
Catullus of the future
young man, your poems are assured,
but your heart – *your heart!*

Anne Beresford

Ariadne in Naxos

And there she sat
her toes covered in sand
staring at the waves
wondering why he'd sailed without her

Her thoughts led her
through caves of betrayal
back to this beach
with its pink shells
coloured stones
and turquoise sea

She held no thread
no hope of rescue
How could she know that the god of mirth
had chosen her
to be caught in his cloud of love
and crowned with seven stars

Untitled

Seven years I have come here
to wait for her

Trains have passed over the bridge
night and day

She has not come

Seven times she called out
but only I heard her
and only I saw the water become clear

Yes then I saw her
and perhaps she was dressed in white
just at the moment
when a butterfly poised on her hair

Seven times the tree has blossomed
and seven apples dropped into my hands

And she has not come

Sean O'Brien

The Heat of the Day

Deep in the restaurant afternoon, we share
The hypnagogic drowse of smoking cooks,
Their seething pans, the far white gaze of fish
Awaiting resurrection by the night.
Some days we think at first it's tinnitus,
But then, for those civilians who can't take
The noise itself or face its jealous glare,
These proxies of the sun evoke our roaring star,
Its gold and black, its cruel command.
Cicadas have to scratch their itch en masse,
Each breath the friction of a Lucifer
Against the empyrean. Fuming skeletons
Botched up from old cicada-wrecks,
Then dipped in phosphorus and set ablaze
Before the god who never calls or writes,
No wonder if they're mad to keep the faith.
Like nudist zealots on the harbour wall
Who want their shadows scorched into the rock,
In time it might be possible to learn
How not to dwell on ice-cubes or the dark,
But atheists are indoors having sex
By thunderous air-con, while we're marooned
Beneath this blinding canvas, hard at work.
The sun is not quite real, nor this white heat,
Nor the cicadas in their adoration.
We're Northerners. We need rehearsals first,
Improving views of Hell from time to time,
The heat deferred into the grave, the fact,
We like to think, beyond imagining.
So then, let's drain the burning glass
And try with incandescent tolerance to catch
The waiter's lizard eye and beg a light –
A sip of petrol? No, but please, the bill,
Though our incinerated voices,
Flaring white with eager terror, sound
Far distant, like the tinnitus of gods.

Robert Wells

Autumnal

1

The water (that soon will raise its undertone
To a funnelled roar) trickles across warm stone.

2

Only so far you accompany the year:
Let it go on alone now, leaving you here.

Castagneto

A wind-up gramophone among spiny husks,
'*Ti voglio ben assaje*' and '*Vecchio frak*':
Under new green we danced in the chestnut grove
On a dry floor of shed leaves. Below us, past
The trees and paved *salita*, the garden-walks
And low grey walls of the poet's ruined house.
If I had cared about precedents, I might
Have thought of his Lalage, of Tyndaris
Invited from the city. But I had eyes
Only for you, Gianna, Maria Grazia,
And thoughts only of you, twin Graces indeed,
The instigators and leaders of our dance;
As, easily smiling and with quick light tread,
You taught a hobbledehoy to match your steps.

Patricia McCarthy

Mainstays
(Somerset Levels)

to C. H. Sisson

Years the women held them:
turbaries dug by hand deep
as graves after every warp –
pumping legends from sluices.
Scyves marked new mump heads
cut from overcrowded beds

into colours of bog myrtle,
buckwheat, rush, sweet gale:
treasures from thin rhines of seas;
woods shrunk in cotton grass
into the vertebrae of fish,
chronicles in sphagnum moss.

Years the women shaped them,
draining scripted lines of ditches
into their own silent vernacular.
Under headsquares of days
they specialised – hiling
sods into crosses, beguiling

horizons with their druid art.
On water-tables they dried
their hearts, standing them on end
widow-dark on the brown
which, lifted into ruckles,
unearthed villages and towns.

Years the women kept them:
the commons, free-for-alls –
binding cradles into floats
while rabbits took to the trees
and the sky spread on the peat
its anonymous soaking sheet.

They knew it would not dry.
They would never ask why
as they christened old willows
'black spaniards', 'champions',
silt smeared over their hearts
for more than frost protection.

Years the women held them
back, not the bogs the women.
In touch with wellsprings
of their own, they made use
of withies worn to mourn
their men in a light tight-shorn.

Rivers in their blood
they corseted when obese.
The horseshoe of the hills
they hung from nearby tors.
To none indebted.
No question, then, of war.

Notes:

Turbaries *were rented for a 'term', usually for 20 years, the last 5 years free, often when a baby was born, to pay for the baby's upbringing.*

Warp: *the verb 'to warp' means 'to flood deliberately' (so that silt-bearing water will deposit its silt and the rich aluvium be spread over the fields. It also protects the young grass from frost.*

Scyves *were knives or spades used for heavy work.*

Mumps *were the cubes that the peat was cut into.*

Hiling *was a preliminary drying of the peat cubes and was considered women's work. Cruciform hiles were often made: 14 turfs on the ground in a cross, each arm of the cross being made also into a cross and displayed as a kind of conjuring trick. The hiles stood for about 6 weeks.*

Ruckles: *after the hiling the turfs were built up in a series of diminishing rings, one on top of the other to form a conical beehive-shape, about 8 feet high. Spaces were left so the air could circulate freely and complete the drying of the peat.*

'rabbits in the trees': *in the 1880s rabbits really did take to the trees and men rowed out to capture them when the floods came.*

'withies worn': *willows were worn for mourning a sweetheart or bride.*

'war' *(last line): At Athelney, Alfred wanted to destroy the heathen invader which Arthur had never done. On Sedgemoor, Monmouth's rebellion was the last battle to be fought on English soil. Monmouth failed in his bid for the throne.*

Patrick McGuinness

House Clearance

Turn the key: note how the emptiness accumulates
as you come in; how by being here at all you seem to add to it,

until it fills the corridor with that fermented stasis
you both disturb and add to as you move. Pass

through a second door, a portal of stirred air,
ignore the rooms to left and right and take the stairs,

your shoes dislodging dust that billows
up in tiny detonations. You're walking underwater,

the silt explodes beneath your feet; at first you think you'll drown
but what's flashing through your mind in one

slow-motion scattering of greys is not your own life but theirs.
No matter that you still can't breathe – that's how it's always

been in here: even the nothingness is thick as blotting paper
on which their shapes have spread like ink – must, damp,

the outline of a body sketched in mothballs and almost-
memory. The furniture is ghostly beneath the sheets

but the missing pictures are still there, outlined
in frames of dirt on squares of wall now white as bone

surprised beneath the skin. You were in every one of them.
Now you're the last flame in the grate:
Hamlet in his theatre of shadows, their embers at your feet.

My Mother

How I think about her now is how
a thought is said to cross the mind:
like a bird's shadow as it flies,
dragging its span in darkness along the ground.

L'Air du Temps

Tracing her perfume, link by link of vapour,
through the crowd to where she's not, to where
her scent expends itself in air
I pass through as if the ghost was me, not her.

Sasha Dugdale

'Perhaps Akhmatova was right …'

Perhaps Akhmatova was right
When she wrote who knows what shit
What tip, what pile of waste
Brings forth the tender verse
Like hogweed, like the fat hen under the fence
Like the unbearable present tense
Who knows what ill, what strife
What crude shack of a life
And how it twists sweetly about the broken sill:
Pressingness, another word for honey suckle
But housewives? Has poetry
Ever deepened in the pail
Was it ever found in the sink, under the table
Did it rise in the oven, quietly able
To outhowl the hoover?
Does it press more than the children's supper
The sudden sleepless wail?
Did it ever?
It lives. It takes seed
Like the most unforgiving weed
Grows wilder as the child grows older
And spits on dreams, did I say
How it thrives in the ashen family nest
Or how iambs are measured best
With the heel of an iron on the reluctant
Breast of a man's shirt?

'Lifting the bedcovers …'

Lifting the bedcovers and there
The scent of little bodies, their secretions
Their feet, bellies, mouths and hair
Animals overwintering for the season
Of a single night, and how the air
Surges into, under, like water through the horses
Of Augeus, cold on the sweet, fetid, bare
Skins, and that smell is fled contorted
With a small grimace out out to the spare
Grey morning, all I embrace
Evaporating in the cool earth's care
Less animal now the opening faces
Their clothes lie folded on the chair
They are awake, but unaware.

Shepherds

Late June the ghosts of shepherds meet on the hills
And one has his crook with its musket barrel hook
One carries a Bible, and all wear the smock
And listen out for the little bells and the canister bells
Worn by the sheep and the big cattle, carried by the wind
Which shapes the hawthorn into mermaid's hair and open book.

There are those who died on the hills, and those who died in their beds,
The haloed, who wear a flame about them, were
Asleep in their wagons, the stove door ajar
The oil lamp tipped. And scores stamp
A last ghastly dawn patrol – their crook a rifle
Cigarettes for their bible.

The hills are not high. High enough
To exist outside us, our low troubles
At the school gates the children look up
And see with a shock of memory
That the earth gathers itself
Into another world
One closer to the sky

Once peopled by shepherds,
Who inherited the high roads from kings and saints
As they passed, withy ropes about their shoulders.
Who spoke little, and wore tall hats
Bawled gently at their dogs,
Who were themselves
Creatures apart

Times when the mist comes up
And rolls like weighted grey
Down the scarp, up there
The cars see their lamps reflected back
A metre ahead, and the back of her is silent
But never like a moor, never fierce like that
She'd carry you back to your own gate
On the palm of her hand – not bury you alive.

Her spine is a landshed, and a land of itself
A land of haunches and shoulders, and glistening fields
Impossible that they weren't in love with her
The kindness of her miles, the smalls of her back,
The blazing white of her summers.

The bible is her book: she wrote it for her shepherds
To train them in oblivion and seasons
And the time she knows, the slowest time on earth
She wrote it in chalk, in rabbit droppings, and lady smock
She wrote it in sweet marjoram and she adorned it with bells
And it has no meaning for anyone, except the shepherds
Who are gone.

Tim Liardet

Jalousie

Into the arms of death, she says, into the arms
of another woman—who speaks the sort of patois

which alone could bind him to a pelt of bones,
whose pomp is laughable, her favours anyone's,

whose glad rags tend towards the sluttish
and whose half moon grin, whose long enfolding fingers

combined one night to snatch away her eldest son.
Though her own legs by now can hardly carry her

to the otherwise bare outcrop of her eightieth year
she knows she has to match the slapper in her rags

and wants to buy new clothes, new fancy shoes
into which she might squeeze her water-swollen feet;

new rouge, new jewellery—flame orange silks;
new ear-rings—a crush of gleams however ersatz,

her mascara a sort of drenched French blue.
Voilà! She has begun an affair with the mirrors

by concentrating on that tiny square of face
that she dreams could still be made beautiful,

framed with hackles of hair, a sort of pout, a sort
of staging of mouth which forgets the fallow patch

of hair which even two mirrors, one held in air
and hand, one in front, cannot quite conspire to reflect—

as she applies a line of lipstick to her mouth,
leans in closer, plumps up the hackles. Ready.

Roy Cockcroft

Wet Harvests

Here on the east coast
The wives and mothers
Wanted their men back, to dry out
Under their own rafters,
Once the sea had dropped its cold claim
On their inheritance.
And so when a coble sank
With all hands, was it too much
To ask of the generous waves
To return the hapless dead
To the shores of the towns that bred them,
For burial in calm graves under slack soils,
Where the churches lay anchored
To their beds of simple faith.

But sometimes the tides would hold them back
For weeks. Sometimes the currents
Would swim them up and down the coast
Until they were miles from home.
Strangers would wash up on the beach,
Men that could be kin, but weren't,
Except that under their bleached skin
All drowned mariners are spliced in the blood
With all the wives and all the mothers
And all the sisters and all the sweethearts
Who have the sea-salt flowing in their tears
And far bigger tides in their own breasts
Than ever ripped keel and deck apart
Or shook the arrogance of piers.

To sort Withernsea from Bridlington
The women turned to worsteds
And big needles, clacking post-codes
Into ganseys, thinking the shroud
Into the wool, and teaching their own blend
Of rib and cable to the black-fingered girls.

How their thick ply foiled the sea's sick game.
Now the draggled fleece on the shingle
Had a name. Now the shore crabs
And the gulls could strip drowned men to the bone,
But never pick the parish records
From their plains and purls.

Jean-Christophe Gouzic

Prometheus Bound and Unbound

Night after night on that lonely outcrop
Prometheus had endured alone the gnawing wind,
Sleet, hail; already inwardly his bones had begun to rot
Though by now the eagle had almost become a friend.

And daily this liver grew in size far from
The weaker, hostile stares of men and women
Too preoccupied with their puny lives to imagine
The ecstasy of one who could defy the gods time and again;

For this is what happens after the sickening trauma
And dislocation and shock and self-discovery;
It is never who we consider we must obey or disobey
After the talons dig in, and the blood seeps out of memory.

Tantalus in Tartarus

When Tantalus first saw the grapes
He fled, stumbling in terror.
Cracked, salt-coarsened his lips
Trembled as at an image in the mirror.

Months, years had passed, thirst
Stung in his gullet like a snake
Whose first bite could prove fatal;
Which fear would never slake.

A Jumble of Letters by C. H. Sisson

Perhaps out of a habit acquired in the office, C. H. Sisson made and preserved 'carbons' of all the letters he wrote. This tiny selection draws on that stock. From the 60s and 70s onwards his two main correspondents were David Wright and Michael Schmidt. Over eighty letters to the latter appear in *Letters to an Editor*, edited by Mark Fisher (Carcanet, 1989), and for that reason none are included here. Some explanations (and a few missing words) have been given in square brackets, but they have been kept to a minimum.

4 September, 1967

Dear W. S. Graham

Your letter was sent on to me in Dorset, where I am spending a week or two, as I do sometimes. Thank you for it.

It is a satisfaction to know that the poem [*The Discarnation*] has been not only received, but read, and by such a reader. I am particularly grateful for your technical re-assurances. I thought this stanza was all right for the purpose. David Wright whom I think you know (& who is a friend of mine) differed. He thought it was suitable only for facetious verse which this hardly is (whatever else). But I think the argumentation put him off too, which I can understand.

The folly of printing this myself is precisely because it will not appear in my next volume [*Metamorphoses*], which Methuen are producing in (they say) January. Perhaps I may (not looking for kind words but by way of thanks) send you a copy.

Yours,

14 Nov, as I suppose, 1971

Dear David [Wright]

It seems that Associated Book Publishers had not yet quite got round to destroying *Art & Action*, so it is to be kept till next year as promised. They had however taken it off their list & are now putting it back. As to *Christopher Homm*, that was just a mistake of the royalty department. As well one as another.

I have picked out Cliff [Ashby]'s 25 best poems, but have heard nothing since.

100

I have a little job. A man called Bernard Lafourcade, writing believe it or not from Carthage, has written to ask me to do an article on Lewis for a special number of the Paris review *L'Herne*. He has read *English Poetry 1900-1950* – at the instance of [Cy] Fox, I make no doubt – and my article on The Politics of W. L. in the late *Agenda*. I am still working out the exact approach but I think of something called *Wyndham Lewis's Study of Himself*, starting from the essay in *Men without Art*.

There was a sort of exhibition here yesterday, mounted by the landlady of the Black Swan (in aid of chairs for the parish room) of photographs & other relics of Langport in the old days. The old days were mostly from about 1890, and the exhibits included a speech of Adolf Hitler, 'dropped by Jerry on Aller Moor', – an improbable way of bringing the war to an early conclusion, one would have thought. There was however also a Langport farthing minted in 1667, and cannon-balls found on the Somerton road. The last-named exhibit sent me out this morning, after some study of the six-inch map, looking for the site of the battle of Langport (1645). I think I see it precisely now, with Goring's men on a ridge to the east of the town, overlooking a wide, gentle declivity with a stream in the bottom of it. It was a wet summer, I know, and Cromwell's men are said to have fought their way up the hedge-rows from which Goring's musketeers were hoping to catch them in a cross-fire. I am afraid the Ironsides were too good for Goring's men. Goring himself is said to have been suffering a lot of pain from earlier wounds, and to have been drinking more than the best generals do. Anyhow they had to fall back on Bridgwater, firing Langport in an attempt to delay the pursuit. The local clubmen – not members of the Athenaeum but locals armed with clubs who had a bash indifferently at both sides, making what they could no doubt & I suppose saving what they could of their own property – joined the winners as practical men will & helped to harry the retreat, although Goring had bought them many a pint at the Langport Arms, in the hope of keeping them sweet. Now I had better have a look in the London Library to see whether my picture of the battle accords with that of the experts. Did you know, by the way, that after Naseby the New Model carried out a once notorious massacre of women – camp followers and ladies who had been helping in various ways, no doubt? – the sort of thing which the less efficient side were in the habit of avoiding. When it was just the odd woman that the New Model wanted to hang up, they were in the habit of discovering that they were witches. Charming days!

It was of course Cromwell who discovered the Final Solution of the Irish problem.

Yrs

Dear David

I was fairly right, but some hundreds of yards out as to the centre of gravity of the battle. Though not I think so far out as my authority (one Col. Burne) would maintain. For he puts the scene of the 'passe' where the crucial charge took place on the present Langport-Long Sutton road. He then has to explain away why there isn't much of a hill at that point; he says that contemporaries did not express themselves very well. I think that a certain track between hedges, and ending in a field, marks an earlier road up over the hill, and that the area of the present road was then probably wooded. Indeed I think the whole course of the brook which divided the two forces was probably pretty well wooded, and that that would account for the concentration on this muddy road, which was practically a 'tunnel', it seems. My authority is interesting as to the manoeuvres immediately preceding the battle, and gives Goring a much better write-up than is usually done. He was badly outnumbered, and my authority explains what usually passes for Goring's half-hearted move towards Taunton as a feint which did, in fact, succeed in drawing off 5,000 of the Fairfax-Cromwell outfit in the wrong direction. It is true that the party employed in this feint were caught with their breeches off, bathing in the river ar Isle Brewers, & fell back in some disorder on Langport. But Goring went out personally to meet them, turned the retreat, sent back the slowest elements first, and brought the rest back in good order. He said the officer in charge of the Isle Brewers affair 'deserved pistolling' – but the man was his brother-in-law, and the unmilitary decencies got the better of him. The battle was largely decided by artillery, Fairfax being much stronger in this respect bombarded the Royalist position until their only two guns – presumably covering the famous road, wherever it was – were out & then sent in his cavalry like a column of tanks. I am sure my friends fought like gentlemen but in the end they had to fall back through the town to cross the Parrett bridge & make for Bridgwater down the old road on the other side of the river. Goring himself, no doubt with some others, withdrew along the ridge on this side of the river & reached Bridgwater that way, much relieved to find the rest of his troops (or those who were not manuring the fields) had already arrived. I imagine that he was cut off from the east gate (still there) by Cromwell's horse & could not get back to the town. This in itself would suggest that the battle spread out a bit further north than Col. Burne suggests (& were not cannon-balls found on the Somerton road?). I shall have to go over this ground with my neighbour the general, who is a writer on military matters and will certainly have considered the matter.

I do not know why I should tell you all this in yr far northern marches. I think in order to repair any damage I had done to the character of the lord Goring, may his soul rest in peace.

Yrs

3 Oct 74

Dear David

Once more in this island, determined not to listen to the babble of your politicians but to cultivate my garden, which needs it. We had an interesting trip, lacking however the great emptiness which I prefer. After the three days at Aix we were taken to Cotignac for the week-end, then put on the train to Arles, where our American friends turned up on the following day and we wandered here and there in their hired car, the whole area which had taken me weeks to explore diminishing in a flash to the size of a pocket-handkerchief. Anyway I saw again Tarascon, Beaucaire, St-Rémy, St Michel de Frigolet, Avignon, Maillane, the Baux and the Saintes Maries. I am now familiar with it, and no longer see it as represented in certain poems – an advance towards ridding my mind of this illusion. 'What infuriated Maurras, when he was finally released from prison', as one of my learned informants said, 'was not that he was not allowed to go back to Martigues but that he was not allowed to go back to Paris.' 'He accommodated himself very well to the life of Paris.' This was an immensely informed and very intelligent young man (I mean about 36), who will I imagine one day edit the authoritative edition of Maurras's work, if the Centre Maurras, which is at present only an association of interested people holding occasional conferences and publishing papers, succeed ever in producing such a thing. Then there was Georges Souville, rather older, the secretary of the Centre, who invited me to take the place of the late Montgomery Belgion on their international list of vaguely associated persons which I think I shall do, the group being reasonably free of those political furies which I should wish to avoid like the plague. He also gave me the names of several academics in the U.K. interested in the subject & I might perhaps get in touch with those at Bath, Oxford and London, just to see what is going on if anything. Anyway these encounters in Aix were worth something. Then Nora and I went one day to Martigues, where I had been told I could freely consult a set of the *Action française* newspaper. It was a pouring wet day. After sheltering for an hour in a scruffy café we had to make the last part of the journey by taxi. The taxi-man re-acted uncertainly but somewhat sharply to the name of Maurras, saying pointedly he was at the Chemin de

103

Paradis 'until the liberation.' (He can have been there only occasionally.) I asked if the driver had known him. He said No, he might have seen him, but he was only a boy at the time. I thought he might be taking me for a boche so I explained that at that time I was myself in the English army – not that that is necessarily a recommendation – and that I was far from wanting to meddle with French politics. We parted on friendly terms but that might have been my modest tip. The maison Maurras was completely shuttered and locked. We wandered round the side till two puppies came out from a shed to play or investigate. After a bit the old gardener, the gardien as he is called, shuffled out. He must have watched and waited for some time before doing this. I reminded him we had met before; he naturally did not remember. I mentioned the name of the man in Aix who had given me to understand he was well known there and that Vasquez (the gardien's name) would let me browse if I said I came from him. He did not remember the name of either of my informants, but finally opened the door but not the shutters & we were in the study or perhaps it was the dining room, or both. He asked me *which* years I wanted to consult, so I said 1908 (the first) and 1940/41. He produced 1908 very jealously and sat down on the other side of the table watching every move as I turned the pages. I read a bit but it was clearly not going to be possible to do much. I had considered coming for a day or two to Martigues, if it had been worth while, and spending a few hours each day browsing. Clearly he was not going to let me out of his sight or even beyond arm's length. Thinking he perhaps wanted to be sure of a tip, which I would have given him at the end anyway, I put a note on the table. 'What's this for?' he said, refusing to pick it up (I left it of course and no doubt he picked it up all right in the end). He asserted that he would not take it. Moreover that if I had come from Martigues he would not [have?] let me see anything, but he realised that I might perhaps want to consult the paper. But he said more than once it would take a long time to read all those papers. There had been a man (I imagine my Victor Nguyen, whom I had met in Aix) who had come for a week and stayed from 7.0 a.m. to 8 p.m. each day, eating his lunch there at the table. But he had had a recommendation from the *patron*. Who was the patron, I asked. He looked surprised that I should not know & said it was Monsieur Jacques Maurras (nephew). I asked if I should write to the patron, and he brightened at once. If I would leave my address, and at the same time write to the patron in Paris, the patron would write to him and then he would leave me to browse as I liked. This it seems is what is needed. I felt so sorry [by hand in the margin: 'or merely that my own situation was so awkward'] for the poor devil guarding his treasures that I gave up – couldn't do much anyway – and shook hands and left. When we came before I caught sight of two figures before we came into the garden. Perhaps one of them was the patron, who visits occasionally, and Vasquez felt safer on that account. Perhaps it was partly the weather; Provençals seem to need the sun. And then on my first visit I was asking for nothing in particular. Probably I shall never go back there but I will write to Jacques Maurras. The papers can be extracted from the British Museum, if I should really want them, but that is a bore. At present I am too uncertain as to the shape of the book to know what I shall need.

Hope all is well in Braithwaite.

Yours

[by hand:] Nora sends her love to Pippa and hopes all is going well.

13 March 75

Dear W. S. Graham

Your letter makes me much regret that I did not call on you when I was in Cornwall a few weeks ago. I thought of Madron, but did not get there, wondering anyway whether you would want the odd stray visitor at some probably inconvenient time. But I dare say you would have put up with it.

David Wright has written a good poem on Bryan Winter's death; he is a man for elegies you know. Roger Hilton meant more to me; not that I ever met him but I greatly admire his painting and in particular his drawings, of which – I have just counted them up – no fewer than eleven hang on these walls, as well as an abstract (a perfect green blob and line) & a blue nude. Most of these were bought when I was working in St James's Square for a huge salary and could go to the Waddington Galleries in my lunch-hour, but I did in fact buy one drawing from his last exhibition, a marvellous charcoal of two nude figures. The first I ever had was a charcoal whirl or whorl of 1960 with a couple of lines underneath: that show was my first introduction to Hilton; what took my eye most quickly was a fish in colour but it had been sold before I arrived; the whorl is marvellous however. All these things retain their freshness for ever & I don't know that you can say more than that.

I was intrigued by what you say of the Canadian poem, and look forward to it knowing that it will be one of the few poems now being written that I shall be able to read. I have just read again your 'Hilton Abstract' & begin to see a connection.

I have recently done a small sequence or rather a group of poems which Peter Scupham is going to set as a pamphlet [*The Corridor*] a bit later in the year & that I will send you when the time comes.

105

All good wishes & regrets for not calling. If ever you are this way, come here. If for example you go up to London by train I could collect you from Taunton and re-deliver you at that station.

Yours

8 January 76

Dear Mr [Theodore] Hars

Many thanks for letting me see your translations. Donald Davie had indeed spoken to me about them. How far I can be of help I do not know. My own approach to the problems of translation is a rather personal one. I am not really a scholar. I did six years' Latin at school, then dropped it in favour of modern literature and languages, and took up the practice of translation from the Latin poets mid-way in my own career as a poet, initially as a form of technical training and gradually as a mode of literary operation. What I have done, therefore, is closely related to the development of my own poetry – and less so, some would say, to the originals. However, you clearly understand this sort of ambiguity, for as you say your versions 'vary in their freedom'.

The one I like most among your versions is Horace *Odes*, I, 10. The reason for this is rather the comparative directness of the language than anything to do with the accuracy of the translation – though there may be a connection of course. 'And roared with laughter' for *risit Apollo* is at once apt in modern speech, and literal.

There are a number of places in the other versions where I feel – maybe wrongly – that you have not stood back far enough to express yourself freely in your own language. Maybe wrongly – because I may be feeling uneasy about things which may be quite legitimate and represent merely differences between your usage and the insular speech to which I am addicted. But take Horace IV, 7. Can 'resumes' be right for both 'grass... fields' and 'branch... leaves'? If the branch resumes its leaves then the fields should resume their grass, and not vice versa? Or what about 'recede' (like the tide from a shore), when what is happening is that the water has subsided so that it flows peacefully between the river-banks? And why is the Grace 'unrobed' – surely not the natural word in American any more than in English – when she is just – all three are no doubt – naked? 'Mortality is this year's tableau' I find awful; it is at any rate inexcusably less *direct* than *immortalia ne speres monet annus*. 'Spring overgrown by luxuriant summer' is surely the wrong image; does not Horace see rather the luxuriance of spring trampled underfoot by the

106

scorching of a southern summer? (That is rather a different sort of point). Do not 'the bars of Lethe' suggest somewhere where drink is served rather [than] translate *vincula* for the 20th century?

I, 3 reads much better, to me. It gives the movement of the whole much better, I think, and the English reads as if you had something consecutive to say. I stick a little at 'dissociating cleave', a pleonasm and a clumsy one. But the language of the ode as a whole *has* movement. In fact in spite of what I said on p 1 I think I like it as well as I, 10.

Of the other pieces I hardly know what to say. I suppose really I think you have been too ingenious. It is rather as Dryden said, a matter of 'dancing on ropes with fettered legs'. There ought to be some more powerful reason for choosing a rhyme-scheme or a form like your tercets than an attempt 'to do something interesting with meter', for metre is interesting only if it is necessary, one might say inevitable. It is not merely not fair on Catullus to twist the last line of 13 to something about a Persian in a tent (it is not as if we cared about Persians in tents), it is depriving oneself of the whole point of reading him if one does not even *attempt* the directness of which he is (with Villon) one of the great masters: 'totum ut te faciant, Fabulle, nasum'.

I dare say you will think some of these comments a bit rude, and of course you don't have to agree with them if, on reflection, you don't. I should like to see Horace I, 10 and I, 3 in print and these I will send on to Michael Schmidt with a recommendation that he use them in *Poetry Nation*. The others I am returning to you, since you may be able to place them elsewhere, if you want to. I don't know whether you will see *The Poetic Art*, my translation of the *Ars Poetica* topped and tailed with introduction and notes and so published at the end of last month by Carcanet, but perhaps what I say there would be some sort of background to these comments. Anyhow, pardon what is excessive and go on as you think best.

Yours sincerely

C. H. Sisson

21 September 76

Dear David

It is no doubt time this correspondence about Cronin's book [Anthony Cronin, *Dead as Doornails*, 1976] came to an end, more especially since you are mainly in the right of it, which is awkward for me: but why you shd attribute to me vulgar errors about the roots of drunkenness I do not know. Or rather I do. But there are other places than Soho where this instruction is given. In my case they include Berlin in 1934 and Abbotabad in 1944. I know nothing of French writers – except their writing: but bugger the literary scene, other things go on in the world which matter even to writers, or ought to.

I have noted in my diary 15 October, the Gods [David Wright's collection *To the Gods the Shades*] to be ready: to enquire of Michael [Schmidt] for that would be the best moment for putting my request to John Gross [editor of the TLS]. Yes, 'Another Part of the Wood' [an essay by Wright published in PN 4] is worth keeping in mind, in this connection.

I was in the Rose & Crown at lunch-time and someone was telling how he ought to have won £30 on the Pools the week before only he had made 'a little mistake' in where he put the tick; he could have done with that £30 to buy two tyres for his car. Ginge (who shoots foxes): Well, you want to win £75,000, then you could have a new car. No, said the other, he (the car) wouldn't turn in here then; he'd have to go down to the Langport Arms, 'where all the Rovers are.' Also learned from another how that calf was like jelly; wouldn't walk, ad to carry im all the way. From Tom Rees how a man at Pitney had been poisoned by thorn apple; and the doctor had said, Well, I haven't seen you for 28 years and now I don't know what's wrong with you. How one as a boy rang the cathedral bell in Worcester Cathedral (which he shd not have touched) and so was the first to ring in the peace, 11 Nov 1918. Thought you'd like to know the latest news from the main news-room.

Cannot say I altogether care for that book (*Anchises*) now it is there. Am tired of the author; and there is too much of him. I think there is more of the real world in *Numbers*, but it seems to escape me now: old age. Dreams, reflections, communings with the same tedious, bellyaching author, that is what we get now-a-days. But there you are. There is a certain performing skill, here and there, I suppose, but what is that?

I think the Basilisk trouble [a reference to Dante?] is going to take a bit of time to sort out. I hardly know what to do; if I intermit for too long, I shall never go back to it. In a way it would be a joyous thing (for a moment) to throw it all over; but then I remind myself that it was a pleasant enough occupation, which took up time & reduced thought to a minimum.

Yrs

14 October 76

My dear Clare [Holland]

If you are nearly twenty, then I am nearly a hundred. Or so I feel after reading your letter and poems. I expect you will think me a very ill-tempered old man, but it is not only age, for I remember what I was doing at twenty, and though you may think that it is so long ago as to have no bearing on the way they do things nowadays, I am not so sure. Indeed it is the whole point of literature – or a large part of the point – that it can cure one a little of the follies of one's own time, which one imagines at first are not follies. Thus by reading the appropriate masters one can learn that people in Roman times, in the middle ages, or in the seventeenth century, had quite different – yet related – ways of thinking about things, yet were human, entirely, and as good as we are or, in the case of the surviving master-writers, much better. Why therefore spend your time at the university learning about the rubbish of popular fiction, or the film: both of which you will get to know something about anyway, whereas you won't get to know the real writers, WHO ARE DEAD, and without whom you will have no standard by which to judge the living, if you don't begin to come to grips with them while you are a student. Ah, good advice. How horrible!

I propose to be rather severe about your poems. For you are no longer a child, yet – I grow more horrible every minute – you write like one. First, there are too many big ideas – this is especially true of 'A Personal Question'. A fatal defect in any writer, in prose or verse. The first thing is to be able to perceive the limits of what you actually see, smell, and feel yourself. All this cant about what God ought to be doing is beside the point. Also, never mind what *they* can do to the scent of a rose, wonders of science and all that rubbish. What if anything do you really want to say about the scent of a rose as you perceive it? Nothing perhaps. Or perhaps some small, definite thing. Secondly, you are careless about rhythm, which is really the key to poetry. You have to listen for it very carefully. It would be a good exercise not to use free verse at all, for, say, three years. Learn to manage the standard forms of stanza and couplet. It may be hard, but any 'free' verse worth calling verse at all is harder still, though I think your metrical education has not yet reached the point where you will understand that. There! Harsh words, meant to be helpful, however, not offensive. The proper use of words – which is what literature is – is a matter of arduous discipline; let no-one persuade you that it is not. That is not to say that poetry, when it does come, may not come 'as easily as the leaves of a tree', as Keats said. But this is not the same as just opening the mouth.

Apologies, and love

20 October, 1976

Dear Dame Janet [Vaughan]

I don't know whether you will remember me from the days when we occasionally sat on the same Civil Service Commission boards.

I am writing merely to tell you that your fame has spread to the Rose and Crown at Huish Episcopi. I say merely, but really that is a distinction, for the Rose and Crown is a very distinguished pub, which first had a licence in 1649 – or was it 5? – and which has been in the hands of the same family for well over a hundred years, the present aged licensee having married the landlord's daughter, after the first war. Into the tap room on Monday – there is no *bar* – came Charley Richardson, part-time postman, building worker, handler of barrels for the Rose and Crown, clutching his copy of the *Daily Telegraph*, for he is an intellectual and reads it assiduously. After some preliminary enquiries about the Edict of Nantes, as to which I was able to satisfy him, he suggested that we should celebrate the birthday of Dame Janet Vaughan: it is apparently his custom to comb through the birthdays to find one worthy of a pint. So we drank your health, he in Eli's powerful cider and I in the excellent Badger draught. I am bound to add that Charley Richardson was under the impression that you were an opera singer of some kind, and it may be of course that you have this distinction too, unknown to me.

Greetings from the past and all good wishes for the future.

Yours

C.H.Sisson

11 May 77

Dear David [Wright]

We went to lunch with Alf (Sacred River) Tomlinson yesterday, in his marvellous retreat at Ozleworth, which is easily accessible on the motorway; and afterwards made a slight detour to look at Combe Farm which the tomb-stone says was the home of my maternal ancestor buried there in the 18th century, John Worlock of Combe Farm. It is at the side of a steep narrow lane, on a piece of ground banked up behind a wall perhaps twelve feet high: a large, square, comfortable-looking house with big eighteenth-century windows and patched up with cement on the walls, with a rickety 19th-century structure by way of a porch. A working farm-house still, not

110

tarted up, even in this Cotswold area of money and refinement. But the fascinating thing is its fortress-like, almost impregnable position, at least from the lane side. It looks like a very old site, and one wonders how many generations of Worlocks lived there, for there are said to be many buried at Ozleworth, even though only two or three tombs are now findable. One day I must exert myself, and look at the Wotton-under-Edge parish register, if they have old ones.

Another canto [of the Dante translation]; still, I fear, less interesting than some. But Pound says in his essay on Binyon, 'after a dull stretch, canto 25 picks up...', so better go on without too much discouragement. I think the trouble is, the last two cantos centre on the devils, and the devils are not as interesting as the damned.

Have you received a propaganda sheet with an impassioned article by Peter Redgrove, saying that those who can draw at school go to art schools, at public expense, and learn from artists, whereas those who can write have to go to stuffy old universities; & there ought to be colleges where they could express themselves and, incidentally, the Literary Creators could pick up a living teaching them?

Yrs

26 June, 1977

Dear Elizabeth [Jennings]

It was delightful to get your new book of poems [*Consequently I Rejoice*] and I have been browsing over them with great pleasure. You write with such ease and confidence, or so it seems – if I know anything of the process it seems so only to the reader. But it is the achieved lucidity that matters, and you *are* lucid – a quality I aim at above all others and seem to achieve less and less.

The borderland between religion and mythology is only one of your territories but it is one where I feel I meet you occasionally. But really the scope of the volume is what impresses, with people seen and books read as alive as your own thoughts. I envy this familiar touch, but it eludes me.

When I came back after a few days away, there was that pamphlet of jubilee poems, and even in that difficult context you have written naturally.

Love

15 July, 1977

Dear John [Campbell-Kease]

Your letter and your folder of poems arrived when I was away in London, or you would have had an acknowledgement before now. I have been browsing over the folder since my return. It would, I think, be best to have a talk about the poems; whether it would turn out to be beneficial, I cannot say – I am very hesitant about the business of indicating what roads people should follow, in poetry as in other things. Most advice turns out to be bad.

Perhaps the most useful thing would be to try to talk about the fundamental poetic which underlies the poems. This would largely be for you to do, for there are different ways of writing, and one can only go on from where one is. I did not mean, in that preface [i.e. the Foreword to the poems in *In the Trojan Ditch*], that facility is a good thing; only that, when it comes, one has to find remedies against it. Yet it is true, as Keats said, that 'if poetry does not come as easily as the leaves of a tree, it had better not come at all.' This is the sort of paradox one works in, I work in, anyway, and all I can do is give you news of my own proceedings. You say you 'have been writing for about a year' and you 'enclose a few'. But you enclose a lot, by most poets' standards; one wonders what your total output is, and how you come to write particular poems, when you do write them. I'm afraid all this must sound vague and silly, but there is a fundamental question of how one distinguishes the real moment of composition from other moments which resemble it; and the true words of the poem one has to write, from others which may present themselves. There is, so to speak, the psychological trick, and there is the technical proficiency; the poem is there when somehow, one manages to subdue a bit of one's technical knowledge to the psychological necessity. I told you I shouldn't be very helpful! I am probably only making the subject more obscure. Or, alternatively, saying nothing which is not blindingly obvious. But you have said it yourself: it is 'the poems which cannot be written' which matter; they are the *only* ones, really.

Should we meet in Dorset or would you and your wife come here for a meal? Perhaps you could give us a ring some time, to fix something. In the mean-time, I hope I may keep the poems for a further browse.

All good wishes

Yours

11 September 77

Dear W. S. Graham

Implements in Their Places is a marvellous book. I don't think there is any of it that is away from the sleight of your true hand, and of what other poet's book, for many a year, can the like be said? Hardly a one.

More than anybody, you seem to have that determination not to speak – well, not to publish – until you have heard the authentic word, which is also the authentic rhythm. I imagine it is, really, not to speak; I only say 'not to publish' because that is all I know. But I cannot imagine you emitting much in the way of loose writing, even for destruction at Madron. Tentative bits, perhaps, when the voice seems about to become audible, but does not quite. Anyway, all you have put in the book is IT.

I remember sending you *The Corridor*, and *The Poetic Art*. But did you ever get *Anchises*? If not, it was a confusion, which would be put right on receipt of a post-card, saying No.

Hack on.

Yours

13 October 77

Dear David [Wright]

I am delighted to hear that the affairs of Bongate are going so well; these things are never without their doubts and agonies. But it sounds to me as if you are now well on the way there.

I know more and more churches are locked, and I know why. Still I think that a remote church, rarely used, had better on the whole be left stripped and open to the world... at any rate if that means the fripperies are not left there, no harm done. I know there are limits to this suicidal policy; but it is, really, the ecclesiastical insurance people who have been campaigning for closure. The church at Cerne Abbas (not remote, certainly) has a notice in the lady-chapel which says that a burglar alarm is fitted to the altar, or words to that effect: whenever I go in I turn that notice to the wall. Still, better churches should be damaged occasionally than that they should become like masonic temples, though the wilder visitors – and not only they – have little enough idea of what happens in them. The other day

All Saints was visited by a mini-bus full of (most orderly) people who I swear, from the cut of the beards, and the serious aspect of the ladies, were *humanists*. Out of a habit acquired when I was church warden (& more particularly during the interval when the living was vacant) I went in. They were exploring the place with knowledgeable architectural eyes & I very demurely offered to show them the 12th century sculpture in the choir vestry. They swept me aside as if I had been a clergyman, native, or other form of low life contemptible to good men and waved their books, in which it was all recorded; less civility than from rampaging bands of cyclists, such as I have met there before, who literally had no idea what the font was used for.

I would expect that you could more easily find Gingers [Ginger is a local mentioned in other letters] in your part of the world than here, where we are not as modern as the eastern counties, but getting on that way as fast as our terrain and the distribution of property allow.

Here are two more cantos (13 & 14): you asked for them. I agree with your comments in general but ask you to consider Yeats's 'Since nineteen hundred nine or ten, Pavlova's had the cry' – which no doubt is Dante's *grido*.

It occurs to me that with canto 16 of the Purgatorio I shall be half way through the *Commedia*. At times the burden and folly of the enterprise, with a language I do not know, (but then, I don't *know* Latin) strike me with immense depression – particularly the burden, for as to follies, if it were not that it would be another. But I suppose I shall go on, from mere habit, thanking God when I am through Paradise.

Yrs

9 November, 1977

Dear Peter [Jones]

I have been reading *The Garden End*, with considerable pleasure, which is something I only rarely get from new volumes of poems, these days – or perhaps any days, truth to tell. Your book certainly has a rare clarity and delicacy. It surprised me to learn, from the Note, that it was reviewers who impelled you to study the Imagists, for I had always supposed you had, so to speak, always been at home with them. Anyway, there was a natural affinity, in your starting-point, and I always feel that if there was *a* right starting point, in the twentieth century, it is/was there, or round-about. For somehow the

114

broken-down machine of verse has to be stripped down, before the engine can be started properly. From there one goes where one can, or where one cannot help going.

The book is excellently produced, with its lovely Girtin on the dust-cover: which I suppose you chose?

There can be few such concentrations of poets as now exists at 266 Councillor Lane. I hope the cat keeps her end up.

All good wishes, and congratulations

28 December, 1977

Dear W. S. Graham

I wish I had something sensible to send you, but there is only this, from two days ago

Leaves are plentiful, on the ground, under the feet,
There cannot be too many, they lie below;
They rot, they blow about before they are rotted.
Were they ever affixed to trees? I do not know.

The great connection is from the leaf to the root,
From branch, from tendril to the low place
Below the burial ground, below the hope of the foot,
The hand stretched out, or the hidden face.

On all occasions, or most, remember this:
Then turn on yourself like a small whirlwind of leaves.

But I am far from sure that that last line will do.

Be that as it may, I have, abashed, to thank you not only for News of Madron and a photograph of W. S. Graham engaged in an inhuman exercise, but for that marvellous leaf of a letter with the green black and yellow woman: which I shall certainly have framed and hang on the wall of what is called my study, a small room containing too many books, and a pine-topped trestle table with (crossed) legs of elm, a piece of furniture which, when I bought it, was covered in goo and disguised, tho' but imperfectly, as an oak dining-table. Your generosity leaves me speechless, so I will not make a speech. There are a dozen Hiltons about the house, so this green lady will wear her

115

nakedness with equanimity one hopes.
Cleveland on Ben Jonson; but would it were Sisson on Graham:

Let Scriblers (that write post, and versifie
With no more leasure than we cast a die)
Spur on their Pegasus, and proudly cry,
This verse I made i'th'twinkling of an eye;
Thou could'st have done so, had thou thought it fit,
But 'twas the wisdom of the Muse to sit
And weigh each syllable, suffring nought to pass,
But what could be no better than it was.

Yours, with all greetings and prognostications of good work in 1978

29 March, 1978

Dear Peter Wood

Many thanks for your letter, dated 16 March but only just arrived here. I have read your poems, and I can understand your disappointment. Perhaps I should explain that Michael Schmidt is the effective editor of the review [*PN Review*], Donald Davie and I sometimes putting in material and reflections from our respective points of view. I don't myself generally see the poems submitted and wouldn't undertake that sort of editorial work. I don't think – other considerations apart – that a man of 63, nearly 64, is well placed to pick and choose among the work of younger men. This is not modesty but a reading of the ways things work. The 20th century poets who really mattered to me are those who were my seniors, who had preceded me by a generation or less: and the time of their influence was early on. Of course, I like some later work better than others, but that is not the kind of authoritative reaction which is needed if one is to pronounce on one's juniors in a way that matters.

There is no doubt that your verse shows a considerable talent with words, and unusual sense of what verse is – something by no means to be taken for granted. Moreover one can sense a reality behind them. Whether you have actually reached that terrible point at which words are stripped down to do what they will do and not what you want them to do, I think there might be a doubt – but that is to adopt a very high standard indeed (nothing to do with being published in *The London Magazine* or anywhere else), but after all the only standard that matters. But I won't pretend I am qualified to criticise your poems.

116

I am a depressing person to come to for advice, for I gave up writing poetry at twenty, started again in drips and drabs at 29/30, did not continue and started again at about 35; even then did not publish or do much about it except put the poems away in a drawer as they came; and published a first book of verse at the age of 47. This looks in retrospect like patience but is probably only confusion. There is no way but to go on, or rather, not go on except when you are sure it is a poem you are hearing. In the end you may have some work. Or you may not.

Sorry to be so useless. I enclose a copy of *The Poetic Art*, of which the notes are an integral part.

All good wishes

Yours

17 May, 1978

Dear Mr [Mervyn] Jones

Many thanks for your letter of 11 May inviting me to take part in a reading at Sutton. I don't really know whether to accept or not.

I hope this doesn't sound rude; it is not meant to be. Of course I take part in readings from time to time, but I have profound doubts about most of these circuses. Probably the only sort that are worth anything are those where there are a few people who have actually read one's work, think it worth bothering about and might even be curious as to how the poet himself would say the lines. Some of one's work I mean, I am not that exacting! Then I can't see much sense, usually, in setting up three or four miscellaneous people to perform at the same time. Even if one managed to assemble three or four poets worth listening to – a rarer feat than is usually imagined – the chances of anyone – even an expert, if there are such things – taking in enough to make the occasion worth while are very small, I would say. And the chances of any sensible discussion, if there is to be a chance for people to open their mouths, about nil.

With that eloquent paragraph I have probably talked myself out of the invitation. This will cause no offence to me, as I hope none to you. I *could* manage 4th or 6th July, but I would want to know a little more about what is proposed.

Yours

30 June 1978

Dear John [Heath-Stubbs]

It was only the other day that I noticed that with *The Watchman's Flute* were the words: 'With the compliments of J.H.-S.', or I would have thanked you for it before now. I thought my copy had just overflowed from Carcanet's store, as something likely to interest me. But in fact, the book has been around ever since it came, picked up frequently not because I thought I had to acknowledge it but because I wanted another read at it. So perhaps no harm done. And I am still finding things that I did [not?] see the real beauty of (so to speak) on earlier readings. As now with 'A Few Strokes in the Sand', the Higgins 'Elegy' and 'After Sappho' – three things so different, and all so accomplished, that one is left wondering at the continuing variety of your performance. Do you know Yvor Winters's work, which Donald Davie is always trying to promote in this country? I admit to not getting beyond a few specimen poems, which seem to me pretty inept. His work seems to me to be the bogus of which your work is the real, the rooted thing of shapely growth (& sturdy) beside which his looks like a plastic ornament. I perceive now that it is not the happiest form of congratulation to introduce that name, but I dare say you will overlook that. Anyway, many thanks for a book which has given pleasure.

Yours

10 July 78

Dear David

What happiness this will bring you! For it is the last of the Paradiso and, although not everybody would want to read four cantos at a time, when you reflect that, once out the other side… Eighteen months, it has taken, with Plautus [unperformed and unpublished version of *The Rope*, done for the National Theatre] and miscellaneous articles fitted in. That is a boast, though really my main feeling is of emerging into the daylight after an inordinate period; and of course it is not really daylight now one is there. Anyhow I shan't look at this again till I get back from Canada. Indeed I regard myself as retired. You will yourself benefit to the extent of not receiving these all too frequent packages. Once again, to have had such a reader is the sort of thing I have had to give up thanking you for. At the revision if will be of immense advantage to have these pointers; but actually during the process it has been very helpful to see the sort of thing which struck you as impossible, and I must admit I have written the more, not the less, freely on that account, thinking as I risked some enormity: See if David swallows it.

I fear this is tedious stuff, and though on the day one finishes a great labour one might feel privileged to bore other people, what you have suffered already deprives me of that right with you. So,

Yours

24 July, 1978

Dear John [Campbell-Kease]

Coals of fire! I am horrified to find how long your photostat poems have been perched opposite me in my work-room. And this morning there comes your sumptuously-produced *Second Chorus*.

I have been busy, though with self-inflicted labours, mostly Dante. From a first look at your book I can tell – by the quality not the quantity – how much work you must have put in and I think you have reason to be pleased with the result. And how some of the poems evoke what is surely the loveliest county in England! I begin to have a sense of the man moving around it aided, say, by Waterloo Station or a child peering through its fingers.

You are out in mid-stream now and I can only wish you to drift on. Where any of us gets to, is another matter.

All good wishes

Yours

12 August, 1978

Dear Donald [Davie]

Michael has let me have a photostat of *Three for Watermusic* and I *am reading* rather than *have read* it. That is to say, I have read it three times, with varying results, pausing between the second and third to read the appropriate parts of Metamorphoses V. So you will see I have given it some attention, but not enough (if there were such a thing) for a final impression.

The first reading was a disappointment, because at this stage I gave what is no doubt too much weight to what struck me here and there as infelicities of tone. It was for example awful to begin with: 'Raped by her uncle, horrors!' This strikes me as less awful, on later readings; but still I am not convinced that this lady-like comment from the twentieth century is quite the way to open the spring for us. Indeed I didn't think and don't think, that (i) [of 'The Fountain of Cyanë'] does justice to the fable, for after the cry in the first line it turns too much to the book rather than to the myth as it wells out of the ground. And I think

And her guffawing Ma assumes the land

intolerable: I do not say you cannot say that but you don't have to – and that, surely, is the test? And is

Wholly a female occasion

in (ii) happy? There are other – to my mind – errors of (I suppose one would say) taste (if taste were not out of fashion). I'm not sure that the word 'epiphany' (such a nice-sounding word) does not come in this category (iii). Ditto for 'game' and 'gamesome' (or only or especially the latter). In fact (iii) I find hard to swallow, except for the purely descriptive or presentational bits. I don't moreover like the intrusion of the talk about rhyme-schemes (the assertion in the first stanza I don't understand, perhaps that's why I don't like it; the statement in the last stanza I think I understand, but am not sure whether those who missed the flash of a fin by keeping their eye on the rhyme-scheme are meant to be as wicked as I think they must have been).

The beginning of 'Wild Boar Clough' makes a good, though what strikes me as a pre-conceived, point; but the general impression, at any rate at first, is again of an intrusion of the literary man.

In (i) of 'The Fountain of Arethusa', have you twisted the legend? No doubt you are entitled to; perhaps there is a reason for it not evident to me in reading. But surely it was Proserpine Demeter was upset about?

Those trivialities said, I have to report that on the re-readings the poem improves a lot (I am slow to assimilate new work). One becomes aware of a deep movement under this surface. It is here that the real interest of the trio resides. I don't, myself, find the recollections of the thirties, with De Reske and Bunny Austin, imaginatively very imposing; and I am not sure that the Shelleyan section of Arethusa *quite* comes off – though I have to report improving reactions with it on re-reading: I think you have to demonstrate, in the surface of the poem, that

These are the springs that matter

rather than flatly say so. And again, the critical dictum about rhyme-schemes (again!) in (iii) of Arethusa seems to me out of place, and to show too much concern with methodology when your point can be proved only by the presentation you in fact make. (But it may be merely that I don't understand what it means, and I don't.)

To me, so far! the core of the trio seems to be in

Gratitude, Need, and Gladness –
These are the names of the walker.

I like the tone and lift of that too; it seems to me that here the spring wells up.

I have talked too much already, allowing myself to put my worries rather than my praises; and I am conscious that I am doing little more than expressing the involuntary reactions of someone whose method of working – and the nature of whose productions – is somewhat different. For what I *think* I see here is a highly worked surface fixed like a grill – if I may so explain myself – over the deep movements of the spring. I can see something moving there, the water, but only between the bars of the grill; and I would rather see the whole surface of the water and what is reflected in it. *Perhaps* the grill will melt like Cyane on further readings; but that is as far as I can report at the [moment]. I hope you will forgive what may seem churlish in this letter – which I dare say is a good deal of it. Anyway, I am immensely grateful to have had the chance to see the poem; I will persist with it.

Finally, it may not be irrelevant to my reading or mis-reading that for me the *Four Quartets* are a come-down after *The Waste Land* and *Sweeney Agonistes*.

And, of course, despite my nigglings, the *Three* is an achievement of importance and a work of profound echoes.

It was good to see you here & I hope it will not be so long before we meet again. Meanwhile, all the best.

Yours

Dear Cliff [Ashby]

Any idea that I was feeling umbrageous about your reference to 'The Cobblestone' [poem later published in *Exactions*] – if that is what is implied by your talk of 'the Cobblestone episode' (I did not know there had been one) – is far from reality. Of course there is a lot in what you say about the monotony of my themes. Like you I write the only poems I can, that is all! Try the poem in last week's TLS. Or don't. Of course like everybody else I like to be over-valued, but I do not think I am badly addicted to poetic reputation, by the standards of many who operate in the field of verse-production. I seek to pass the time, and at this I think, from what you have said from time to time, that I am perhaps a little better than you are. My occasional feelings of guilt in addressing you are from awareness that, if I am better at it, it is not due to any merits of mine but, first of all, to that fact that I am better off than you are, secondly, that my early interests and I suppose you might say education were such as to make it natural for me to write articles about this and that, edit or introduce the odd book, and generally amuse myself like a literary old gentleman of a type more or less passé (though I do not really belong, socially or otherwise, to that type, which anyway had largely disappeared before I got there); thirdly, through a mis-spent life (but all lives are mis-spent), I have habits of industry or at any rate flapping around which, God knows, are common enough in one field and another.

It is maddening about Hodders remaindering I.T.V.T. [*In the Vulgar Tongue*, 1968] without telling you; but publishers at large seem to be very off-hand about the usual clause in agreements which says that in the event of the book being remaindered the author will be given the opportunity, etc. I had this trouble with Granada about *English Poetry 1900-1950* (which I often want a copy of but can never lay hands on one), and with Faber over the *Case of Walter Bagehot*, though in that case some were recovered from the remainder dealer. With *English Poetry* there is the further annoyance that it was published also in America (with bound-up sheets from here), where there were said to be 'a Year's supplies' (no doubt at the back of a ware-house somewhere) and I have never been able to lay hands on a single one.

I can believe what you say about the relative advantages of council estates and cottages not fitted out with mod. cons.; though something must depend on the area, I suppose? And above all on size and lay-out? There are certainly one or two small groupings round here which *look* all right, certainly no worse than some estates built by speculative builders. I am so lucky in this respect that I scarcely dare open my mouth. But am I contented? With the house, Yes, but with Life, No. Never have been, really, and now that I am old – a lot older than you! – what can you expect?

Enough of this. Glad to hear Ann is better.

Yours

16 October 1978

Dear David

The Spender/Bergonzi review is excellent; never have I seen so much sense talked about the thirties in so small a space (or any space). So you will find nothing instructive written on it.

I waved to W Cookson (now rather fat) at the party but did not speak to him. I have, however, since had a letter from him which I enclose. I have not accepted the invitation to write about *Tenebrae* because, after all, I have written at length about Hill, even mentioning some of the poems in the new volume (of which I have an inscribed copy, dated in Vancouver). If only Geoffrey could shake off his literary preoccupations. A line like

Married, and not for love. You, of all people!

stands out with touching clarity (and rhythmic splendour) in the midst of more considered matter. Or so it seems to me. He is probably a simpler poet that he makes out, and a simple poet is a very difficult thing to be, in these times. Still, his poems did stand the test of being listened to a number of times, and even the elegant explanations he repeatedly offered about the *coplas* were pleasing as a thing in themselves, though I came to feel that there was too much explanation for those skimpy pairs of lines. Brian [Patten], by comparison, – his work rather – did not improve by repetition and one learned to shudder at the approach (yet once more) of 'Angel-Wings' or 'Into my mirror'… Yet he has a true vein of lecherous sentiment, a little too pathetic and self-regarding:

sometimes I think a boy's body would do as well:
Sometimes I think, my own might do.

It usually does, one gathers, so there is no need for the catch in the throat. There was a wonderful bit of comedy in Ottawa [during a British Council

123

tour involving the three poets]. After a post-reading party in Montreal, in one of the university common-rooms, Brian was taken home by a smashing young woman, all smiles and bosom. Next day, in Ottawa, there was a great box of flowers waiting for him at the hotel. (If you knew Brian you would understand that it would be this way round.) That afternoon we were to go to a party at the house of the British Council representative. It happened also that Brian knew, in London, the son or daughter of one of the university staff who was going, with his wife. So Brian whipped off the name outside the box and took this parcel with him to the house of the British Council couple, Geoffrey in alarm lest our hostess should imagine the flowers were for her! And perhaps, he speculated afterwards (not without envy), there was a tender note inside. Brian's comic poems are very good entertainment, the first time of hearing. There is one about the remains of poets in the university of Texas, or somewhere.

Do not be appalled by anything you have ever said. As a matter of fact, I think *The Corridor* is probably all right, as a *ne plus ultra* of a kind, but little excuse for going on belly-aching after that. However, the most hopeful reform *is* silence, which will come later if not sooner.

So taken with the stream of my eloquence, I have said nothing about the poem on MacDiarmid which, however, I had read twice on first opening your letter. Have since read it again. I like its gentleness and mistiness – well, it is not exactly misty itself but it does conclude marvellously with the curtains being drawn. Also the

> like him I am not hearing
>   the keen of the pibroch

is, so to speak, a piece of remarkable friendliness in place of

> like me he is not hearing

which is the form one would expect [David Wright was deaf].

Yours

Dear Sydney [W. S. Graham]

Roger Hilton's green girl continues to wave her arms at me from the corner of the room, and to wear her hair like a hat. From time to time I have said to myself (useless to speak to her), What *can* I send W. S. Graham as a sort of present or counter-signal? No answer. Then I thought, One could always send a few bottles of whisky for Christmas. Then the many difficulties of this operation began to overwhelm me, till I thought: Whisky is good but money is even better, for it transfers the problem thinking and acting from here to Madron. I hope this will sufficiently explain the enclosure.

I hope the rumour is true that Fabers are to produce your collected poems in the spring. This will be something. One ought to be able to go back and forth a little more easily: and there are all the innocent young who have yet to notice this remarkable lump of poetry.

David Wright, who saw your interview with Penelope Mortimer wherever it was, says: 'I admire the exquisite technique it exhibits, how not to answer vulgar impertinent questions while pinpointing their impertinence und vulgarity, all without impoliteness or offence.' By the way, I am sub-editing a thing for PNR for David's sixtieth birthday (February 1980, which means doing something in the first half of next year). I will write to you about this when I have got organised: but I hope you will be willing to do something, perhaps about the early days, for I gather you have not seen him since the fifties.

All that is good.

Yours

28 April, 1990

9 April, 1990

Dear Neil [Astley]

If I were stuck in a lift with either Mrs Thatcher or Mr Kinnock I hope I should be able to get in touch with an engineer. As for advising them on the nation's business, which they understand so imperfectly, with all the advice they have already ….. Or pretending that I understand it myself…

It was certainly a brilliant idea to publish a volume of letters [*Dear next Prime Minister*, 1990] to these eminent persons; the only trouble is that I am hardly the person to write with even a fictional conviction that I could do either of them any good. In real life policies and opinions are all my eye and there are only practical problems and a perpetual competition to misrepresent them more or less.

I fear I wouldn't fill the gap you have for 'what people now think of as old-fashioned Toryism', though I'm a bit vague as to what that is. I am for what is left of the Constitution, as I hope we all are, though nobody thinks about it much now. Not a party man at all, though I have voted for both in turn, neither has given satisfaction. Naturally all those years in and around Whitehall add a touch of professional scepticism, and I shouldn't anyhow expect satisfaction from such a quarter. The best thing to do with a government is to put up with it.

Sorry not to be more illuminating.

Yours

30 August, 90

Dear Rob [Stuart]

It would have been a pleasure to hear from you anyway, but the remarkable invention that accompanied your note is in a different category. I have read it several times, with increasing interest, and I think you really have done something. Only resist the temptation, and go on to something different when the time comes – the temptation, I meant to say, of repeating these effects. Anyway I am delighted that, having achieved this, you thought of associating me with it. The Pessoa fits without jar, and prepares the way for the final reflection.

I am glad to know that your work is developing so successfully, which must mean that you have the all too rare gift of waiting instead of rushing to fill a volume as the vulgar do. I apologise for these pontifications, but you know that the old are given to advice they have never followed themselves as rigorously as they should have done.

How are the family? Is there any hope that we shall one day see you all in these parts? Life goes on much as you know it here, allowing for the usual declensions. Note how tactfully the type goes fainter here, in sympathy.

Again with many thanks, and with all good wishes.

Yours

Dear Harold [Pinter]

My wife and I saw *Party Time* on Monday, and indeed we took the daughter and son-in-law whom I think you may have met at the South Bank. It certainly cleared my mind on one thing: it does make a difference to see the play on the stage. The disposition and movement of the bodies seemed to be integral to the text – not always the case in my admittedly scanty experience of the theatre.

What struck me was how much this increased the force of the sort of reference to events off-stage which of course is not new to your theatre but seemed in *Party Time* to be exceptionally powerful. I found myself wondering what sort of link there is here with the old classical convention that little more than vestigial actions are allowed on stage, and that all has to be indicated in words and gestures. You do not eschew violence on the stage, but to me one of the superiorities of *Party Time* over *Mountain Language* is that so much more is entrusted to the words. If I may make a niggle – it is no more – about the presentation of *Party Time* it is that your businessmen types would have been more rather than less effective if they had not *looked* so patently unpleasant. After all, being pleasant is a crucial part of business, and a little more plausibility, contrasting with what an attentive listener would get from their words, would not be out of place. But who am I to speculate on how audiences take things? I suppose it was right, in the general context, to present Jimmy as the utterly innocent victim; it certainly made for a dramatically effective contrast. But really, of course, there is no such person and I was left with the impression that the final scene risked turning the play too much into the conventional revolutionary myth, coming not so much from Karl Marx as from Jean-Jacques Rousseau.

You will know how little attention to pay to these reflections from so unqualified a source. They all come from a wish to see as much as possible to be left to the author's language, and the total effect of the performance was to enhance that hugely, which I suppose is not more than to say that for me, having read the play before, it passed from the extremely interesting to the profoundly dramatic. Such commonplaces!

With apologies for not having something useful to say. And many thanks for a memorable evening.

All good wishes

22 December, 92

Dear Kate [Hooper]

It is certainly not an inconvenience to me, that you should propose questions about Dante and his influence on English poetry. Whether I can answer them, in a way that will be of any use to you, is another matter.

It was, actually, Michael who rashly and – as I thought at the time – foolishly, first suggested that I should translate the *Divine Comedy*. I seem to remember that it was on an occasion when I met him at Taunton station, to bring him here, and that I replied rather briefly and rudely. However, when he had gone, I tried my hand at a few lines – I had long messed around with various bits of translation: it is not really, in my view, altogether a bad habit in a poet. Contrary to my expectations, a long labour followed.

This was, however, far from being the beginning of my interest in Dante. That can be dated more or less precisely, from my second year as an undergraduate, when I acquired a copy of Eliot's essay on Dante. Universities did not 'teach' Eliot in those days; I had discovered him for myself. From the time I read that essay, with its memorable quotations, I never lost sight of Dante, but it was several years before I followed him up with any extensive reading. I had a few elementary Italian lessons soon after the war began, I imagine, to help me with the Temple Classics volumes – with *en face* prose translation – which I had acquired. Anyway the Temple Classics *Inferno* volume went with me as far as the Arakan and was occasionally even read at, here and there.

How has Dante influenced me in my own work? Hard to say; I am a practical poet, rather than one who thinks about things. But from the first encounter, in 1932, that clarity and one might say luminosity of that line, its sinuosity and force, lodge itself in my mind in some sort of way. How far this had a bearing on my giving up writing poems at the age of 20, and my unpremeditated – and slow – return some years later, I have no idea, but so far as, then and later, I showed any tendency to scrape my lines bare, my guess is that Dante had a hand in it, though it would be unrealistic to think of it as entirely separate from other influences: I suppose the best simple guide to the influences would be the authors recommended in Pound's pamphlet, *How to Read* – not that that was final or exclusive. Nothing is.

I am glad that you found you could read my Dante. It was anyway an invaluable occupation, to sit down day after day, following or rather accompanying the poet on his journey and trying to say in my English, however faintly, what he had said. With Dante – as in turn with Catullus, Lucretius and Virgil, my translation has been a matter of belatedly coming closer to a poet whose works I had long known something of, and found particularly valuable. Leisure has been rather scarce, for most of my life.

It is possible to find odd traces of Dante here and there in my poems – as in 'Cato' or in a phrase like 'straws in glass' in 'In Insula Avalonia', or even in the form of latter, but I should think that the poet's temper and interests have mattered more. He is very much a man who has lived in the world and not in one of those romantic shelters many of the poets of the 19th century (and later!) thought up for themselves and for the comfort of their self-esteem.

You say that you believe the *Divine Comedy* to be as relevant to the 20th century as to the Middle Ages. I am sure you are right, if by that you mean that the view it gives is concerned with the permanent features of human nature, and with the concerns which are proper to it. Where Dante points, there is always something there. He includes so much that, when it comes to talking about 'influences', it is hard to say how much it is he who has operated on one and how much one has acquired from other sources. I hope I have not put this too obscurely: what I mean is that pre-war Paris and Berlin have more to do with my view of politics than Florence, and the England of the 17th century more to do with my traces of theology than St Thomas Aquinas.

I'm afraid that none of this will help you very much with your thesis. It is an interesting subject, and I wonder what you are finding on the way. I should like to have talked to you about it, if Manchester had been a little nearer. I imagine you are unlikely to come to these parts, but if you do, let me know. In any case, I wish you well with your thesis, and your final year in general.

And, in view of the date, a happy Christmas and all the best (including a good degree) in 1993.

Yours

David Constantine

Hölderlin Fragments

1

> *Sweet then to live under the high shadows of trees*
> *And hills, sunnily, where the way*
> *Is paved to the church. But for travellers whom*
> *For the love of life, always measuring,*
> *The feet obey, the ways*
> *Blossom more beautifully where the roads …*

The trees reach for the sky, the hills even more so; the church itself, fastened hard on the ground, points upwards. And you have settled for the one path from house to house, from yours to His, and can tread it dryshod any afternoon to botanize in His sunny acre and continue your family history among the lichened and leaning stones. Meanwhile every April roads to the four quarters clothe like girls in plum and cherry and quit this hollow and lead out over the hills and far away.

2

> *But*
> *Through the garden slinks your fearful*
> *Guest without eyes*
> *Madness. For the way out*
> *Will hardly be discovered now by anyone*
> *With clean hands.*

Not that long ago – the Golden Age ? – it seemed the garden was the best place to be. High wall around, savagery outside. And here they are in the Age of Lead wondering how to get out and madness playing blind man's buff among them. State of siege, the supplies eating up, madness as contagious as the plague. And as to clean hands, have they forgotten what they did to make this place? They dunged the ground with blood and bone.

Now the wilderness is waiting. It has patience. It has learned all it needs to learn about the human race. When the cleverest finds a way out of the poisoned garden and calls to the others, Tool up, lads, and follow me! the wilderness will be waiting. It will eat them.

3

But when the busy day
Is lit
And on the chain that leads
The lightning down
The heavenly dew of the hour of rising shines
Then feeling climbs
High in humans too
So they build houses
Work starts up
And shipping on the river
And men and women offer their hands
To one another, give and receive, sense
Is earthed and for good reason then
The eyes fix on the ground.

Earth, we assume, can take any amount of lightning. The spires reach up for it and hand it down and in. A phenomenon! Very exciting. But I know people – not many but enough – who seeing the morning dew in everyday radiance don't know what to do with themselves. None of the usual trades will satisfy. I might say beware the hand of a man or a woman reaching for yours with that sort of light in his or her eyes. Then you'll need earthing, the pair of you. Eyes down, the earth can take it. Doubtful if you can any more.

4

But I am hummed about
By bees and where the ploughman
Makes his furrows the birds
Sing on the light. Heaven
Has many helpers. The poet
Sees them. Good
To hold on to others.
For no one can bear life alone.

The beauty of it, that friendly interacting of earth and air and the creatures of earth and air, is also a rightness. Indeed, this fitting together helpfully may be that without which there can be no beauty. The parts fit, they belong and work together, this may be the seed of life in the making of beauty. The beautiful poem is a living example of mutual aid. Even Heaven – this poet says so more than once – needs helpers. So saying, he revolts against the very idea of omnipotence. He extols the cosmos, the dance, the democracy. The part is no good on its own. It makes no sense. It is not viable.

5

Above all spare
The wilderness made
By gods and decreed
Clean to their children to walk in
Among the rocks as they please

Perhaps after all it would have helped to believe the earth didn't belong to us. The mistake was putting us in charge. So easy for our kind to pass from that to thinking we owned the place.

Heatherlands bloom
In purple for you
Lady and dark springs too
For you and your son but for
The others also

The other gods and goddesses and their progeny. At the start there was a good deal of commingling and nobody bothered much who your mother and father were, god and goddess or one or the other with the woman or man next door. All we had to do was not trash the place.

Or the gods will take back what is theirs
By force, as they would from serfs

Too late now. Masters and slaves. But all the four rivers of paradise, confluent and directed, will hardly wash the wilderness clean of us.

6

Terrible therefore over the earth
Diana, huntress, walks and angrily
The Lord lifts over us
His countenance brimming with
No end of signs. The sea meanwhile
Sighs when he comes

Implacable when outraged, sister, don't forget, of Apollo who stood by the ships and loosed the arrows of plague into the packed army of the Greeks, she, Diana, Artemis, huntress, walks the earth and does not like what she sees. And over the rooftops, hills, forests and out of the level sea the flat white face of the Lord himself is rising. Now even the stupidest know what he means. The oceans, three quarters of the surface of the globe and increasing daily, sigh. Still, view things anthropomorphically if you must. Say that the salt water, out of which love stepped, sighs with relief that now it will soon be over. Not even the stupidest will suppose that the waters are sighing in pity for us. But relief or pity or the murmur of awe at the advent of Artemis and the Lord – all nonsense. In truth the sighing is the seas coming to the boil.

Meanwhile let me walk
And pick wild berries
To quench my love for you
On your paths, o earth

You might walk to botanize or to see the world or to lay your worn-out boots on the altar of Saint James in Compostela. Surely not in the wish to quench your love. Besides, earth whets the appetite she feeds. Walking her paths and browsing on her berries won't quench your love for her. And why should you wish it would?

Late summer, the paths are open, the berries are plentiful. Enjoy the meantime. Walk, eat while you can, shut-down and dearth are coming. And of course this may not be only the usual winter. Perhaps the wish for quenching is pre-emptive, to suffer less. Perhaps he is thinking, I'll walk while I can and browse on the berries of the earth and pray I can walk and browse so much I'll have had enough and staying at home under the clock tower in the everlasting winter will be bearable. Lessen your love, grieve less.

This bright morning, I'll think the meanwhile is meant to last for quite some time and that the lover's purpose in ambling and striding out in it is to prove and be glad of what he knows already about his love. He is lean and alone, he carries very little, he strides along, he feels on a day like this he could walk for ever. His mouth is stained with berries.

Note:

I modelled these 'Hölderlin Fragments' on Hölderlin's own Pindar-Fragmente *which he composed in 1803 at the time of his beautifully strange versions of Sophocles' Oedipus and Antigone. Each of those nine texts consists of a fragment of Pindar's verse, closely translated into Hölderlin's own late language, and a passage of prose set below it as though to explain and comment. But that comforting relationship – text + exegesis – is belied by the practice. Out of the fragment of a poem, elusive in its peculiar beauty, Hölderlin derived a poetic prose which itself reads like translation from a strange elsewhere and itself seems to call for exegesis. The whole sense of each piece is generated in the interplay of ancient text and modern reading. Resisting exegesis, they reach out from the borders of his alienation for future readers to continue them.*

I translated my verse fragments from among the many poems Hölderlin began and could not finish in the four or five years after the death of Susette Gontard and his being taken into the clinic and then the tower.

Josephine Balmer

Two Versions and an Original Poem

Ovid's Pupil

(from *Tristia* 3.7)

Among dictionaries, lexicons, you will find her –
go on, seek her out, hastily-scribbled letter;
whatever she's doing, whatever she composes,
she will put aside to hear how her dear friend is.
Ask her if she still follows our uncommon pursuit,
still works away on her own verses, if all Greek.
'For you', please say, 'are modest as well as beautiful,
with the rare dowry of wit, literary skill.
Yes, I saw the flame in you at such a tender age,
when I played father, leader, poetic comrade.
So if you still burn with that fierce, all-consuming fire,
only Sappho herself can ever burn brighter.
In different times we read our work, each to other,
often I played critic, judge, as well as teacher.
I offered a keen ear for all your fresh-hammered verse;
when you stalled, stuttered, I could make you blush.
Lay down your fear, Perilla, Poet, Scholar, arm your heart,
return to sacred practice of our noble art.
Your loveliness will be touched by old age's damning hand,
creeping up with relentless step, without a sound.
And when they say 'oh she *was* beautiful' you will grieve,
complain it's your mirror that now betrays, deceives.
You have talent in some measure, are worthy of more;
mould it, shape it in your soul to a boundless store.
For Fortune gives and Fortune takes away, as she pleases –
a beggar today, yesterday rich as Croesus.
So you, for whom a promising life of writing waits,
take heed of the coming pyre, make verse your escape.'

Perilla's Legacy

In Rome he barely spoke, or not to me;
I was just the girl who came with mother.
In exile everything changed. Suddenly
I was 'Sappho', *poeta, doctissima,*
promising pupil who could live forever.
True, I loved clothes, my face in the mirror;
I knew, as he pointed out so kindly,
that my hope, at best, was mediocrity
(he claimed his criticism made me blush –
try hiding away for days, crying, crushed).
Still I burned with that same flame, I thirsted
for fame, hungered for crumb of genius,
all feint praise, the promise that would curse it.

But he played with me and the more he toyed
the more I faltered, confidence destroyed
until lines dried, hunger eased, fire was damped.
In the end his conceit left only this:
the stale kiss of indices, appendix,
Classical Women Poets, Non-Extant.

Petronius's Chalice

(from Tacitus *Annals*, 17.18-19)

He had devoted his life to feasts and sensual pleasure.
Nights were his days, not dissolute but voluptuary.
His chalice, they say, worth 300,000 sesterces,
and cast of blue john, mined only in Britannia –
that rare and precious stone all drunkards pray for –
ensured the more he supped, the more he sobered.
It seemed he had known it was waiting, Nero's envy,
the betrayal that bequeathed brutal ultimatum:
arrest, disgrace, or flick of knife on opened vein.
They say he lay down calmly as his blood ebbed,
entertained his loyal friends, hospitable as ever,
talked not of the life to come, or of philosophy
but gossiped, joked, read from his fine *Satyricon*.
Sometimes he slept, rehearsing the hush of death
but made no Will, refused to weep or beg or flatter,
listed, instead, Nero's lovers: Male, Female, Other.
And so his enemy could not claim or pollute them
he destroyed his signet ring, all prized possessions,
took one last sip then watched his chalice shatter.
In every shard now he saw the shrouded Peaks
and shivering myrrhine mountains, Mam Tor
flecked with flinty rain, sharp as arrow shafts;
the corroding course of lime-washed streams,
jagged like a heart-line, life about to splinter,
fading away beneath in half-remembered dream.
He walked towards it, that soft northern pass.

Note:
'Ovid's Pupil' is a fairly 'straight' translation, if condensed, of Tristia *3.7 while
'Perilla's Legacy' is an original poem in response, opening up a dialogue between
text and original. 'Petronius's Chalice' blurs translation and original; the first half is
loosely based on Tacitus* Annals *17.18-19 (plus a bit of Pliny's* Natural History *37.7
– and some help from a small leaflet for ASD Jewellers of Castleton, Derbyshire) and
then the final part of the poem is my own. Such work explores the borderlines, the
cracks between translation and original, allowing each to illuminate the other. Such
poems could not exist without a close working knowledge of the source text yet do not
feel constrained by it, instead allowing it to operate as a creative stimulus; the nets,
to misquote Joyce, by which we fly.*

Five Tanka

Translated by Timothy Harris

    Had I the time
I should go and gather
    lost-love shells
which congregate, I've heard,
on the shore at Suminoe

Anon (probably 8th century)

*

    The one who first
lifted my jet-black hair
    while I lay there
careless of its disorder –
my heart, how it aches for him

*

    I never weary
of putting into words
    things I recall:
the water in my inkstone
is nothing but my tears

Izumi Shikibu (?976-?)

*

    The axe bites
and odour shocks the sense –
    the grove in winter

Yōsa Buson (1716-1783)

*

The melancholy
of living among the hills –
  to whom shall I tell it?
Gathering goosefoot in a basket
going homeward as light fails

Ryōkan (1758-1831)

Three Haiku

Translated by Harry Guest

June rainfall constant
        just on one night
        moongleam through pines

                        Ryōta (1718-87)

                *

Alone again after
the firework display.
Starless darkness.

                    Shiki (1867-1902)

                *

Unmoving river
a summer sunset
        boat tethered
        rusty iron
        glints in the water

                    Yamaguchi Seiishi (1901-94)

Heinrich Heine

Translated from the German by Terese Coe

Where?

Where at last will this wandering end
and a quiet place be marked as mine?
Under palms in the Southern sun?
Under lindens on the Rhine?

Will I be laid in a shallow grave
in a wilderness, by strangers' hands?
Or find my rest near breaking waves
under a long expanse of sand?

It makes no difference. God will wind
his heaven round me there as here,
and like the lanterns of the dead,
at night the stars will hover near.

David Cooke

Sea Breeze

after Mallarmé

The flesh is weary. And books, I've read them all.
To fly away, escape, somewhere, like a bird
that's high in the rush of spray and foreign skies.
And what's to keep me here? Nothing. Not the grace
of formal gardens that once assuaged the eye,
when now the oppressed spirit seeks its sea-change –
not nights when the desolate glare of a lamp
is reflected in the blank intractable page,
not even the mother nursing my child.
And so away! The creaking masts are calling.
Weigh anchor for hallucinatory lands.

Mortal tedium, so often deceived by hopes,
still needs to believe in the handkerchiefs waving
their last goodbyes, though bound perhaps for shipwreck
I may be lost at sea, and far from fragrant islands –
But, O my heart, just hear how sailors sing!

Vasco da gama

after Mallarmé

Fixated on travel, beyond
even India's resplendent sprawl,

let this verse be the messenger
that brings you word of fame –

as when, on the lowest yard
plunging with its caravel,

a proclamatory seabird
skims ecstatically the spindrift,

shrieking forth its news
of futile bearings, despair,

and the night sky studded
with gimcrack stones –

while the helm holds steady
as your own imperturbable smile.

Stoics

after Máirtín O'Díreáin

Our fathers, and theirs too
who came before them,
found themselves at odds with life
in the struggle
to coax their native rock –

content at least
if dour skies relented,
and a shallow field
brought forth
its meagre crop.

To build a dike
or a drystone wall
was each man's stoic pride –
as a poet makes verses
to keep his language alive.

And we now
who are their children
lodge in city rooms
where a landlord might charge you
to fix his leaking pipe.

Yet even we
will be remembered –
for the paperwork
we've left behind in our loathsome
government office.

Mario Petrucci

Salt Flat

after Jacques Prévert, 'Sables mouvants'

Bedevilled marvels
Zephyr & tide
Now retired the far neap
& You
Bladderwrack embraced so breezily
Among quagmire sheets you fetch up dreamy
Demonic wonders
Onshore – offshore
How far that spring already wrenches
Through half-cut eyes
Two little swells remain
Wretches & wonders
Wind & tide
Two ripplings that drench me

Robert Desnos

Two Poems translated by Timothy Adès

Beautiful After-Midnight

Whiter than the snow or the crystals of salt
Flowers of night are spreading wide their petals
Growing in the sky to fill the spaces of the vault
Where a blue horse neighs, kicks, heads for meadows

And grasslands sown with newly minted stars
Through harvests of pinpoints and reflected light
Spattering the sails with its four horseshoes' flares
Plunging in deepest shadows milky-white

Rolling out the ribbon of rhythms long since dead
The shortest buckling with the weight of day's last fire
Suns paled and faded that went too near the red
Glow of the constellations Hercules and Lyre

Even now the moon who is robed as a bride
Drags in her white claws the misty one and white
White as the morning on ocean petrified
The ram of the dawn prepares his dashing flight

The comet is wearing its sparklers on its brows
You moon black and beautiful moving slow ahead
Where do you meet your golden-plum-eyed spouse?
With a splendid body Venus warmed his bed

You champagnes go streaming through the constellations
If wines are similar to liquid stars
Then Burgundy in you let's recover the creation
Of fairytale monsters, the ether, empty spheres.

Cancer and the Bear, Mercury and Jupiter,
As we press the vintage we shall make them shine
Never mind the sun bathed in fresh spring-water
Never mind the torches reflected in the wine

Beautiful after-midnight with the legends in your train
Draw another couple to the waltzes of desire
Till the weary drinker shall ask you once again
To fill up his glass with blood of memory's fire!

The Voice of Robert Desnos

So like the flower and the breeze
the stream the passing shadows
the smile glimpsed that great night at midnight
so like everything joy sorrow
it's last night's midnight rearing its naked torso above the
belfries and poplars
I summon those who are lost in the countryside
old corpses young felled oaks
rags of cloth rotting on the ground and laundry
drying near women
I summon tornadoes and hurricanes
tempests typhoons cyclones
tidal waves
earthquakes
I summon smoke of volcanoes and cigarettes
smoke-rings of luxury cigars
I summon loves and lovers
I summon the quick and the dead
I summon ditch-diggers I summon assassins
I summon executioners I summon pilots masons and
architects
assassins
I summon the flesh
I summon the one I love
I summon the one I love
I summon the one I love
triumphant midnight spreads its satin wings and sits
on my bed
belfries and poplars bend to my desire
they crumble they subside
those lost in the countryside finding me find each other again

W. S. Milne

Shadows

versions of airs by Samuel Beckett

i *vive morte ma seule saison…*

alive dead my sole season
white lilies chrysanthemums
quick nests abandoned
mud of the leaves of April
beautiful days grey with rime

ii *imagine ci ceci…*

imagine if this
a day like this
a beautiful day
imagine
if a day
a day just like this
ceased
imagine

iii *fin fond du néant…*

at the back-end of nothing
the eye trusting waits
to glimpse
the head moving slowly
the stillness speaks
but that's only in the head

iv *somme toute*
    tout compte fait…

all in all
reckoning it up
quarter of a millisecond

on the quarter
every hour
not counting
the dead time

v *rentrer*
   à la nuit…

come back
at night
home to light

to switch off to see
to see the night
face
pressed to the pane

vi *noir soeur*
    qui es aux enfers…

black muse
straight from hell
too sharp by half

and cutting
what is it that you want

vii **silence tel que ce qui fut…**

such silence as used to be
never before
never again like that
the murmur torn
from a word
to say too much
no longer able
to go on
vowing not to shut up

TWO CHOSEN BROADSHEET POETS

Sophie Mayer, 32, is the author of *Her Various Scalpels* (Shearsman, 2009) and *The Cinema of Sally Potter: A Politics of Love* (Wallflower, 2009). She is the Books Editor for *DIVA*, a commissioning editor for *Chroma* and a contributing editor for *Hand + Star*. For more information, see: www. sophiemayer.net

The Doctor's Daughter

He
is the first man I ever saw
naked:
shifted between shivering flanks
plain as a table –
      he is a closed system
      shunts and vents
      play the stops
      a watershed
      all run in one direction
an island and
yet –
may not a stranger wash up on his shore?
I would enter his blood like
a pearl of air. No.
      My fingers would trace his
      veins from above like
      clouds returning
      water
to its source.

Hide & Seek

For Abel Meeropol

In slowness, so much hides. The mythic:
I learned the slow way, made a fist

of it. Music was my medium, or the words for it,
and I worked through them. Librettist,

Communist, pseudonym. Stories within stories –
that's what I teach. What they try to hide, you must

find out. Sing out. Put out fires with dirty water,
if it's what you have. Call yourself names. Split.

Play a part. Leftist New York Jew. Bleeding heart.
And where I hid it – in plain sight,

in the long rope of her voice, drawn tight
against your neck. Shivers, people tell me, light

hairs raised. Whoever's singing. But me, I don't.
Work to do, the young to tend. And at the end

of the day, it's her words I take: God bless the child
that's got his own. Own what,

who knows. Perhaps to own a want,
like mine: to hide and be found out.

Of Other Spaces

Tate St. Ives

i

You are a green place
      wild rice and marsh birds
flying the blue horizon
      of the hundred thousand things I will never know
a blur, or curvature
      three times and trembling
against stillness whose
      stone asks after your tongue
the moment where you breathed
      and stopped, a winding cut from the sheet of the world

ii

Did my lover make the curtain? Yes. Between
sculpting and the sea. She made certain. She

occurs in this room. The empty cup. The stillness
of the day. She resonates, is the thickness of paint.

Is white. Yes. My memories are this blue. The sea's
particular invention: to want to see through blue,

whose translucence salts the eye. Taste it. I have never
thought of the sea as my lover. Never thought of her

as a wall. But there it is. And another, and another.
The emptying room. Blazing full.

METAL / steel warrior

after *Zonder Titel* ∞ *VIII,* Maren Dubnick

To begin with, she had
no idea. Just wound: that was the way

of girls. So the songs go. The thread was clear,
the pin sharp: together, they satisfied

her silver eye. Beginning
with the middle, that's where she stayed,

plumping it, with a tapering off
at either end. And as she turned so

on the spindle of herself, she sung –
tunelessly – of body parts, in words

her brothers thought she shouldn't know,
and didn't. Great cascades of flesh

fell from her lips like the hum of
the new looms, her fingers nimble

among them. The thread wound
clear as if to say: nothing to see

here. Her core – phallus, heart or belly – caught
on the point of a steel pin. And so

she turned on her steel spine, pupating,
wound or wounded in her

egg of thread. A silvering, she was,
a lit preciseness, holding open.

Rosie Breese is 26 and lives in Cardiff. She has had work published in *nthposition and 3:AM Magazine*, and *Poetry Wales* (forthcoming). Her poem 'Wrinkles' was recently commended in a competition run by Leaf Books. In September she will begin an MA in Creative Writing at UEA.

Samson

To go back:
the cautious bow
pressing the quiet sea
whilst the sun

shone like an echo.
We two alone

picking over the island. Blistering light
nudging at the blown-dry bird-husks, littering
every path. Angel-fossil.
Foetus. Ammonite

foundations, roofless
cuckoo-mouth agape,
fossilized in flight.

The limpet shells piled high
for sucking: comforters
of soft bile.

And bracken
marching in green heat,
cradling its stone cup
like a child.

The gasping island
drinking the tide,

drawing from the kelp
a tithe of stones.

Some watch like eyes, some watch like bones

the sky tearing down,
mute as fathoms.

Five,

the boat is coming for us.

Note:

An island off the Cornish coast. The last inhabitants scraped a meagre living out of the land, before being forcibly evicted during the 1850s. Local legend has it that the place is now populated by ghosts.

Prologue

Ernest 'Baden' Squelch, my great grandfather (1901 – 1963)

The tiny organ's half-starved cry
pushed you forth. Baden Squelch
and wife, sixteen, hand in hand hastily
creased together in the camera's squint,
crowned with sweat in the century's sun,

forged in a clatter. It has taken years
to unfold. The Morse code: sleep
caught between the machinery of feeds.
For days the rollers' animal roar
chewed the wilful steel flat.

But for those blissful seconds full to brimming,
the way that Friday nights seemed to balloon out.
When your steps were answered by the knock of stone
echoing through terraced canyons.
A loud scattering of stars

now thinned to sonar. Insistent, the cry
with no-one to lift the receiver and press
Cancel. Watching the lips of the mill
spewing out words half-remembered,
bright chunks of metal, narrowed to a dial tone.

And blank screens have rolled out.
You can no longer be deafened. You are
fit for nothing. Afternoons in exile
watching the sun sink beneath the chimneys
sucking smoke through blackened lips.

And your children hobble in shoes too narrow,
training their feet into soft coffin shapes.
Cloistered, you study the glass's spiral base,
head cocked amidst the fog, the roar of engines
listening for the stars' sounds of sorrow

that will bring you home from the asylum.
A miracle you will conceive there
on the white sheet. A malignant proliferation
your lips will not give voice to.
It will be left to the pipes. Their gleaming rolls

will scatter the codes of pain to be born.

Embroidery

Blind, you sit there still
at the single-paned window,
knotting its fern patterns -

the net that caught the stars; slunk
under a grapple of frost
knowing that you would not see

with raw fingers, only feel
their absence: your text,
the shape of your loss.

When I am found

Who are you? they will ask.
The dripping leaves, I will say,
the concrete furrow. I am
here, cold and waiting.

Where have you been? they will ask.
The clouds gathered me
in handfuls, razored me
in slivers, scattered me
in the gutter's black eyes.

What did you leave? they will ask.
I breathed a word, damp in the ear
of each person I met.
Whisper through the walls, I told them;
the mould will speak its mirage
sudden as stars.

How is it? they will ask.
It is like walking on water, I will tell them,
only more miraculous. It is like falling
and flying, depending on the day.

Why all this? they will ask.
There was nothing but urgency.
The eyes of crowds in the dark,
ocean-wide. The harbour lights
out for the night. Mist descending.
Blindness, and the heave of water.

When will you be back? they will ask.
This is when I will surprise them all,
shaking from black feathers
a scattershot of ice, my squawks
exploding softly into cold air then fading
like steam: *Nevermore. Nevermore.*

Notes for Broadsheet Poets

Extracts from C. H. Sisson's critical essays, selected by Charlie Louth

There is no question, as it has come to me, of filling note-books with what one knows already. Indeed as the inevitable facility comes, the conscious task becomes the rejection of whatever appears with the face of familiarity. The writing of poetry is, in a sense, the opposite of writing what one wants to write, and it is because of the embarrassing growth of the area of consciousness which writing, as indeed the other serious encounters of life, produces that one has recourse to the conscious manipulation of translation, as it were to distract one while the unwanted impulses free themselves under the provocation of another's thought. I have come in the end to have great sympathy with Dryden, who having pushed his way this way and that at the end of his days took pride in being able to do a translation better than any of them. He was glad, I imagine, to be able to release the energies of poetry without passing for having said anything of his own. I do not pretend that my path has led me so far. There are other enabling distractions – reasoning and analysis, mythology and other narrative, properly used. All these are really modes of the problem of form.

The claim of a collection like this is in the continuity of statement which underlies the historical recording, analysis or imitation and is recognisable in the development of rhythm rather than in overt logical connections. The proof of the poem – any poem – is in its rhythm and that is why critical determination has in the end to await that unarguable perception.

from the Foreword to the poems of *In the Trojan Ditch* (1974)

*

It is not an impertinence to try to translate great masters. It is a tribute that one pays.
[…]
It is an ineluctable law that a verse translation has to be done in the only verse that the translator, at the time of writing, can make; and that if he could not make verse before he will not suddenly become so gifted because he is faced with a classical text.

from the Foreword to the translations in *In the Trojan Ditch*

*

162

'The poem' is words on a piece of paper, or spoken, just as 'the building' is erected before you and you must make of it what you can. Nobody supposes that you feel what the builder or the architect 'felt', as he sweated through his work, even in cases where there is one man to whom a 'feeling' or an original creative act could with any plausibility be attributed. Of course buildings are in styles as well as being in materials, and many people have a hand in them. And so have poems although one man will, these days, put his name on the title page. Take no more than a due amount of notice of it; it is to get the money, or the reputation, or in hopes of the same.

from 'On Poetic Architecture' (*Essays*, 1967)

*

One should not write more poetry than one must, and some formula has to be found for passing the time between poems. The conduct of affairs is one, though probably not the best. While one is seeing this world, what worlds is one not seeing! But at least these avocations prevent one from thinking of oneself as a poet, which for most writers of verse must be very salutary. The annihilating pressure of work seems an enemy, but so many times of idleness, as a student and in the army, have produced nothing that one cannot say with certainty that relief from this treadmill would produce more, though I think it would. The writing of poetry is a matter of personal economy, but it cannot be treated as such, for one does not know what one wants to discover. One can only go on living, and be grateful for this by-product if it comes. It may be just pleasure, or it may be the truth peeping out.
[…]
The poet has problems which you can call technical, if you like the word, but when he is at work all his problems are one, which is to keep what he is saying within the limits of the perceptible. The words of most of the communications which pass between people cannot be seen, smelt or tasted; they can barely be heard. They are (what is called) understood, by which is meant that they have certain practical effects, as the turning of switches or the movement of gear levers. […] The point is that the poem exists as a natural object exists, so that you can look at it, hear it, smell it, as you can wind, waves or trees, without asking why you are doing so.
[…]
Perceptible literary objects come in all kinds of shapes, and the work of a particular writer, taken chronologically, is likely to show a series of shapes related in the same way as the shapes you might expect to see emerging one after another from a painter's studio. The changes in the series pass for

163

being the poet's development, but how does it look to him and why does he pass from one point to another in the series? He is not ordinarily thinking of developing […]. He is thinking – so far as he can be described as thinking of anything apart from the subject-matter – of making a poem which will not be the same as the last one. The development of the series is in one sense the result of a negative rather than a positive effort. If the familiar presents itself as he feels his way through the poem, he discards it, knowing that it would not be part of the poem, but would be a 'soft' bit. What, through its familiarity, can no longer be attended to, is of no use for his purposes. The unfamiliarity ought to be continuous but it is not absolute. Unfamiliarity is a relative thing. It is related to what is familiar; there is a background of expectedness to all that is unexpected. The poet may change things, but he starts from somewhere.

[…]

It is an absurdity to try to be original. You might as well try to be beautiful or intelligent. But the complementary process of ridding yourself of obsessive influences can possibly be assisted by some conscious effort. A young man, however, cannot shrink back at the first touch of an alien hand. He has to live through his Eliot, his Yeats or whatever it may be. For a time he must wear fashionable clothes. Then he must discard them, and be prepared to find, not merely that he is naked, but that under those clothes he simply was not there at all.

[…]

As a piece of technical advice to the writer: Tell the truth and hope for the best is […] inadequate. Some good writers have been quite extraordinary liars, along certain lines, as for example Ford Madox Ford. The truth is interesting if you can tell it, but the writer will feel a need to simplify his problems by abridging it in some way. What is not so good is putting in phoney bits. This also everybody does more or less, but the better writers less. The advice one might give – if any advice were of any use – might be to write about something about which you have some truth to tell. For the poet the truth is what he can perceive. This is the point at which the technical problems and the problems of subject-matter become the same. But is rhythm a part of the truth? It seems odd to say so. One feels for the subject, and if one finds it one finds the words. But the rhythm? The fact is that you cannot find the words without the rhythm, and what you might call your words, in a borrowed rhythm, would not be your words. So evading other people's rhythm is part of finding your own words …

from 'Natural History' (*Art and Action*, 1965)

*

We all live in a language which brings with it more of the past than we can hope to discern; we have to read the poets of the past from where we are and as who we are. When we speak, we speak as we are made.

[...]

There is a tension between the original author and his translator which involves language and thought and the whole world each of them moves in. It is the establishment of this relationship which so to speak constitutes the moment of discovery in which the poet-translator finds that he can venture on his subject. A great poet – any real poet – is present in every line of his work; the essence of his work can be received in a flash from a single poem or from a few lines, and what follows is a deepening of that insight. The poet-translator cannot begin until he has gone a stage further. He has to find the tone in which he can speak. This is not a deliberate search; it is a revelation which can only come to him involuntarily, as a line of his own may come to him, out of the blue. It must come to him concretely, a few words or a rhythm suddenly emerging, a few lines and – suddenly, he knows how the thing can be done. After that he can go on, through all the intervening hours of labour, to the end. No doubt the quality of the intuition varies, and the work that follows can be more or less true to that initial hunch, but some hunch there must be if a poem in a foreign language is to find a voice in this one.

[...]

A poet will not be tempted to say in verse what he could say in prose, but there will be moments when words come to him in a rhythmic form which will admit of no other way of saying them. It is his sense of the sequence of rhythms which will determine what words he takes and what he lays aside during the process of composition. The sense of language which demands that the choice shall be made in this way cannot suddenly be summoned up by any act of will or by a publisher's contract. The suitability of a specific kind of verse is an expression of the relationship established between the translator and his author, between one age and one language, and another age and another language. What we call a translation is no more than a reading, in one time and place, of a text from another place and time. It syphons off something from the original, but as much only as we in our different world are able to take. A successful translation – the concrete embodiment of a reading – does not preclude other attempts, it invites them. All are partial, all give the original a particular twist. That is why, beside the word 'translation', which implies the removal of something from one place to another, we should set the word 'version', which emphasizes the twist.

from 'The Poet and the Translator' (*In Two Minds*, 1990)

165

*

The first necessity is to have something to say, but even this will be present only as an impending cloud, and to assert its necessity is to make an *ex post facto* analysis. The moment announces itself by words conveying a rhythm or, it may be, by a rhythm conveying a few words.
[…]
Poetry – verse in any serious usage of the term – is a receptacle for sense which cannot be put into prose, and which burdens the speaker until it is said. 'Lully, lulla, thou little tiny child' is a paradigm of the art; the assonance and half rhyme, and the rhythm, are rigorously essential to the meaning to be unloaded. The line says what cannot be said otherwise. Poetry is precisely that; all other speech hangs more or less loosely. Only the greatest poets maintain this degree of rigour at any length.

from 'Poetry and Sincerity' (*In Two Minds*, 1990)

*

These lines (40-7 of Horace's *Ars Poetica*) contain the essential directions for the poet or indeed any writer. Find what you can write about and you have solved your problem. Of course the aspiring writer has to face the possibility that the answer may be, Nothing. At any rate, the beginning, as the continuation, of literary capacity involves a certain self-knowledge. Nothing is further from it, therefore, than the intoxications of publicity and reputation.
[…]
Whether or not the poet can be said to keep the language alive, the language is alive in the poem […]. The question here is what the individual writer can do for the life of the language. If one has not a certain confidence or at any rate hope that he can do something, one has no business with poetry at all. To make the old word new one has only to use it properly. A word not only carries a meaning but derives significations from the context in which it is put. The full meaning of a word in a poem is the product of its history, including the current usage, and its location. How far one can increase the charge on a word by deliberate placing is questionable. Horace is very precise in what he says on this subject. 'You will have said well' is how he puts it – *dixeris egregie* – if it turns out that the way you have placed the word in fact renews it. The novel impression is a critical test you can apply when you have written your poem rather than a trick which can be recommended to anyone wanting to turn out a good one.
[…]

166

The poet should not only give pleasure but say something sensible.

[...]

Pas de perfection dans les arts could be either a statement of fact or an injunction. While Horace has earlier insisted on the importance of revision, he here (lines 340-52) admits that even the best works have faults. He might have said, ought to have faults, for nothing is more likely to kill a work than trying to make it a treasury of individual beauties or smart phrases. Even in a writer of genius, the determination to 'load every rift with ore' – Keats's phrase – impedes that movement as a whole which is the mark of the successful work, as Keats himself discovered.

[...]

What training should the poet give himself? The question is worth considering, even though it is too complicated to admit of a satisfactory answer. The training of an athlete is, after all, only the final polish on a life well-endowed and hitherto well-spent, so far as fitness for a particular range of movements is concerned. What constitutes the 'well-spent', as far as the poet is concerned, is more than anyone can say. It may include the encounter with and solution of infantile and adolescent problems which everyone would avoid if he could. Poetry is so comprehensive in its subject-matter, and its wells are so deep in the psyche, that there is no reason to suppose that the 'well-spent', in the case of the poet, is in general any different from that of the rest of the world. Certainly anyone who seeks to justify particular lines of conduct on the grounds that he is a poet is suspect, if for no other reason than that he will certainly not *know* that what he does will produce better poetic results than the line of conduct that he rejects. [...] One's immediate starting techniques as a poet will [...] be learnt from one's somewhat older contemporaries who may not be very good and whom one will learn to discard and – properly – date one's real start as a poet from the date of that discarding.

from the Notes to *The Poetic Art: a translation of Horace's* Ars Poetica (1975)

167

List of Books and Pamphlets by C. H. Sisson

The Curious Democrat (Peter Russell, 1950) [under the pseudonym Richard Ampers]

An Asiatic Romance (Gaberbocchus, 1953)

(tr.) *Versions and Perversions of Heine* (Gaberbocchus, 1955)

The Spirit of British Administration and some European Comparisons (Faber, 1959; second edition, 1966)

Poems (Peter Russell, 1959)

Twenty-one Poems (privately printed, The Westerham Press, 1960)

The London Zoo (Abelard-Schuman, 1961)

Numbers (Methuen, 1965)

Christopher Homm (Methuen, 1965; Carcanet, 1975, 1984, 1997)

Art and Action (Methuen, 1965)

(tr.) *Catullus* (MacGibbon & Kee, 1966) / *The Poetry of Catullus: a Modern Translation with the complete Latin text* (Orion, 1967; Viking, 1969)

The Discarnation (privately printed, The Westerham Press, 1967)

Essays (privately printed, Knole Park Press, 1967)

Roman Poems (privately printed, The Westerham Press, 1968)

Metamorphoses (Methuen, 1968)

English Poetry 1900-1950: an Assessment (Rupert Hart-Davis, 1971; Carcanet, 1981; Methuen [University Paperbacks], 1981)

The Case of Walter Bagehot (Faber, 1972)

In the Trojan Ditch: Collected Poems & Selected Translations (Carcanet, 1974)

The Corridor (Mandeville Press, 1975)

(tr.) *The Poetic Art: a Translation of Horace's* Ars Poetica (Carcanet, 1975)

Anchises (Carcanet, 1976)

(tr.) *Lucretius: The Poem on Nature* (Carcanet, 1976)

(ed.) *The English Sermon 1650-1750: an anthology* (Carcanet, 1976)

David Hume (The Ramsay Head Press, 1976)

(ed.) *David Wright: A South African Album* (Mantis Editions, 1976) (ed.) *Jonathan Swift: Selected Poems* (Carcanet, 1977)

The Avoidance of Literature: Collected Essays, ed. Michael Schmidt (Carcanet, 1978)

(tr.) *Some Tales of La Fontaine* (Carcanet, 1979)

Moon-Rise and Other Poems (Snake River Press, 1979)

Exactions (Carcanet, 1980)

(tr.) *Dante: The Divine Comedy* (Carcanet, 1980; Pan, 1981; OUP, 1993)

Selected Poems (Carcanet, 1981; 1990)

(ed.) *Philip Mairet: Autobiographical and Other Papers* (Carcanet, 1981)

Anglican Essays (Carcanet, 1983)

(tr.) *The Song of Roland* (Carcanet, 1983)

Night Thoughts and Other Poems (Inky Parrot Press, 1983)

(tr.) *Joachim du Bellay: The Regrets* (Carcanet, 1984)

Collected Poems (Carcanet, 1984)

(ed.) *Christina Rossetti: Selected Poems* (Carcanet, 1984)

The Poet and the Translator (The Sixteenth Jackson Knight Memorial Lecture) (University of Exeter, 1985)

(tr.) *Virgil: The Aeneid* (Carcanet, 1986; Everyman, 1998)

God Bless Karl Marx! (Carcanet, 1987)

(tr.) *Jean Racine: Britannicus, Phaedra, Athaliah* (OUP, 1987)

On the Look-Out: a Partial Autobiography (Carcanet, 1989)

16 Sonnets (privately printed, H & C Laserprint, 1990)

(ed.) *Jeremy Taylor: Selected Writings* (Carcanet, 1990)

In Two Minds: Guesses at Other Writers (Carcanet, 1990)

Antidotes (Carcanet, 1991)

Nine Sonnets (Greville Press, 1991)

English Perspectives: Essays on Liberty and Government (Carcanet, 1992)

The Pattern (Enitharmon, 1993)

Is there a Church of England? Reflections on Permanence and Progression (Carcanet, 1993)

What and Who (Carcanet, 1994)

Poems: Selected (Carcanet, 1995; New Directions, 1996)

(ed.) *Edgar Allan Poe: Poems and Essays on Poetry* (Carcanet, 1995)

Collected Translations (Carcanet, 1996)

Collected Poems (Carcanet, 1998)

See also:

Angels and Beasts: New Short Stories from France, edited by Denis Saurat (Westhouse, 1947) [contains four stories by Jules Supervielle translated by CHS]

Contemporary Authors Autobiography Series, Vol. 3, edited by Adele Sarkissian (Gale, 1986), pp. 293-309

Letters to an Editor, edited by Mark Fisher (Carcanet, 1989) [contains many letters from CHS to Michael Schmidt]

Ghosts in the Corridor: Andrew Crozier, Donald Davie, C. H. Sisson, Paladin Re/Active Anthology No. 2 (Paladin, 1992)

PN Review 39 (1984), C. H. Sisson at Seventy: a special issue

Notes on contributors

Fleur Adcock's new collection, *Dragon Talk*, her first since *Poems 1960-2000*, has just appeared from Bloodaxe (May 2010).

Timothy Adès, born 1941, took a degree in Classics and studied International Business Management. He has won many prizes for his formal translations of Homer, Victor Hugo, Robert Desnos, and for the Resistance poet, Jean Cassou's *33 Sonnets* (Arc). *Agenda* Editions published further translations of Jean Cassou: *The Madness of Amadis* in 2008. A volume of Robert Desnos is forthcoming.

Josephine Balmer's latest collection, *The Word for Sorrow*, for which she was awarded a Wingate Foundation Scholarship, is published by Salt. Previous collections and translations include *Chasing Catullus: Poems, Translations and Transgressions, Catullus: Poems of Love and Hate, Classical Women Poets* and *Sappho: Poems & Fragments*. She has recently been awarded a PhD by Publication in Literature and Creative Writing at the University of East Anglia.

Anne Beresford has lived and worked in Suffolk for over thirty years. Her *Collected Poems*, published by Katabasis in 2006, contains poems from all her earlier books.

Roy Cockcroft is a retired drama teacher living in the East Riding. His work has been published in *Poetry Nottingham, Orbis, Agenda, The French Literary Review*, as well as elsewhere. His poems can be read online at *South Bank E-Poetry* and *Aireings Magazine*. In 2008 he won first prize in the Ted Hughes International Competition with his poem 'Wet Harvests' (included here).

Terese Coe's poems and translations have recently appeared in the *TLS, Agenda* (see the Rilke issue), *Orbis, Poetry* and elsewhere. Her first collection of poems, *The Everyday Uncommon*, won a Word Press publication prize in 2005. She has won several other prizes for her poetry. She has an MA in Dramatic Literature from the University of Utah, and currently teaches English Composition at the New York Institute of Technology.

David Constantine's most recent publications are *Nine Fathom Deep* (poems, Bloodaxe), *The Shieling* (short stories, Comma) and a translation of Goethe's *Faust* (Penguin). With his wife Helen he edits *Modern Poetry in Translation*.

David Cooke was born in 1953 and was a Gregory Award winner for his poetry in 1977. After a poetic silence of about twenty years, he has started writing again. His poems have appeared or are forthcoming in many magazines such as *Acumen, Envoi, The Frogmore Papers, The Interpreter's House, Poetry London, Poetry Salzburg Review* and *Poetry Ireland Review*. A new book, *In The Distance: Selected Poems 1972-2010*, will be published this year by Night Publishing, Hull.

Sasha Dugdale recently translated *The Grainstore* by Natal'ya Vorozhbit for the RSC and Chekhov's *Cherry Orchard* for BBC Radio. She has published two collections of poetry, *Notebook* and *The Estate* (Carcanet / Oxford Poets).

Jean-Christophe Gouzic's poems have appeared in many journals such as *The North, The Frogmore Papers, Iota, Poetry Nottingham, Orbis*.

Harry Guest's new collection *Some Times* is scheduled to appear from Anvil this summer.

Timothy Harris is an actor, director and writer who is based in Japan. He has written for many publications, but has been associated chiefly with *PN Review*.

Tim Liardet has produced six full collections of poetry. *The Blood Choir*, his sixth collection, won an Arts Council England Writer's Award as a collection-in-progress in 2003, was a Poetry Book Society Recommendation for Summer 2006 and was shortlisted for the 2006 TS Eliot Prize. A chapbook – *Priest Skear* – will appear in July of this year. *The Storm House*, his seventh full collection, is due from Carcanet in 2011. He is Professor of Poetry at Bath Spa University.

Charlie Louth's translations of Hölderlin's letters and essays (done with Jeremy Adler) were published by Penguin last year. He teaches German at Queen's College, Oxford. C. H. Sisson was his grandfather.

Patricia McCarthy is the editor of *Agenda*. She has just finished a long sequence, *Lost Footsteps*, mainly in the voices of Rodin's mistresses.

Patrick McGuinness's second collection, *Jilted City* (Carcanet), is a Poetry Book Society Recommendation and his first novel, *The Last Hundred Days*, is out next year. He teaches French at St Anne's College, Oxford.

W. S. Milne is an Aberdeen poet. He has published two books of poetry and a translation of *Agamemnon* in Scots. He has published a full-length study of the poetry of Geoffrey Hill. He is currently translating Aesop's *Fables* into Scots prose, published serially in *Lallans* magazine, and has just completed, in collaboration with Malin Bergman Andrews, an anthology of modern Swedish poetry translated into English.

Victoria Moul is a lecturer in Latin literature at the University of Cambridge. She has recently published *Jonson, Horace and the Classical Tradition* (CUP, 2010).

Sean O'Brien's most recent collection, *The Drowned Book* (2007), won the Forward and T. S. Eliot prizes. His novel *Afterlife* appeared in 2009. He is Professor of Creative Writing at Newcastle University.

John Peck's most recent book is *Red Strawberry Leaf* (Univ. of Chicago Press, 2005). With Sonu Shamdasani and Mark Kyburz, he has co-translated C. G. Jung's *Red Book (Liber Novus)* (Norton, New York, 2009). He lives in Connecticut, USA.

Mario Petrucci's most recent literary project is an epic sequence represented so far by *somewhere is january* (Perdika Press) and *i tulips* (Enitharmon 2010). He has translated Catullus and Sappho (Perdika Press).

Stephen Romer has published four collections of poetry with OUP and Carcanet/ Oxford Poets. His latest, *Yellow Studio*, was shortlisted for the T. S. Eliot Prize 2008. He has translated widely from the French, his most recent anthology, *Into the Deep Street: Seven Modern French Poets 1938-2008* (co-edited with Jennie Feldman), came out with Anvil in 2009. He also edited *20th-Century French Poems* (Faber, 2002). In 2010 he is Visiting Fellow at All Souls, Oxford.

Michael Schmidt at Carcanet has been C. H. Sisson's principal publisher since 1974. Sisson collaborated editorially in the magazine *PN Review*, still edited by Schmidt, who also edited the substantial collection of Sisson's essays and reviews, *The Avoidance of Literature*, and was responsible for his *Poems: Selected*. He commissioned many of the major later translations and has anthologised and written about Sisson's work for three and a half decades.

Robert Wells was born in Oxford in 1947. His *Collected Poems and Translations* were published by Carcanet in the Autumn of 2009.

Clive Wilmer has published six collections of poetry, the most recent of which is *The Mystery of Things* (Carcanet, 2006). He is a Fellow of Sidney Sussex College, Cambridge.

Subscription Renewal Letter

For quite some time now, subscription renewal letters have been sent to subscribers so that it is clear when their subscriptions have lapsed and to avoid confusion.

Please look out for a **RENEWAL letter from World Wide Subscription Service** when your subscription is due again and send in your subscription as promptly as possible.

Remember, 4 issues of *Agenda* comprise a subscription for a year. This could be two double issues, a double issue and 2 single issues, etc.

Do not be confused when, even if you have not yet renewed, you receive the next issue of *Agenda*. It does not mean that your renewal letter was a mistake. We send *Agenda* out in good faith, hoping that when you receive the journal, you will recall the subscription renewal letter you received and be reminded to send in your subscription promptly, if you have not yet done so.

Do not forget you can subscribe by direct debit if that is easier for you.

We thank all subscribers for staying with us and hope to give you many more issues of *Agenda* to stimulate, challenge and inspire you!

VISIT THE WEBSITE

Agenda's vibrant showcase

www.agendapoetry.co.uk

Visit the website for further translations, poems, paintings and essays, Broadsheet 14 for young poets and artists.

Young reviewer/poet Loveday Why's response to the review of Don Paterson by Rory Waterman in Agenda's Fiftieth Anniversary issue

New Poetry by:
Sudeep Sen
Gary Allen
Joseph Allen
June English
Sam Gardiner
David Burns
Wendy Holborow
Paul Robichaud
William Virgil Davis

New translations

Young translator/version-maker:
Omar Sabbagh of Mahmoud Darwish

Essays:
Harry Guest: a Tribute to Richard Burns

Samuel John Perry on Larkin and Edward Thomas

Sophie Hannah on Sisson's influence on her novels

Belinda Cooke on Peter Robinson's new book on translation

TEAR–OFF SUBSCRIPTION FORM

Pay by cheque (payable to 'Agenda'), or
Visa / MasterCard

SUBSCRIPTION RATES ON INSIDE FRONT COVER

1 Subscription (1 year) =

| 2 double issues |
| 1 double, 2 single issues |
| or |
| 4 single issues |
| (The above is variable) |

Please print

Name: ....

Address: ....

....

....

.... Postcode ....

Tel: ....

Email: ....

Visa / MasterCard No: ☐☐☐☐ – ☐☐☐☐ – ☐☐☐☐ – ☐☐☐☐

Expiry date: ☐☐ – ☐☐

Please tick box:

New Subscription ☐   Renewed Subscription ☐

(or subscribe online – www.agendapoetry.co.uk)

Send to: AGENDA, The Wheelwrights, Fletching Street, Mayfield,
East Sussex, TN20 6TL
Tel: 01435-873703

175